BLACK MEN LOVE

A Tribute To Love From The Unique Perspective Of Black Men

By
Kenneth Wilson

Co-authored by Phenomenal Men

2022

A TRIBUTE TO LOVE FROM
THE UNIQUE PERSPECTIVE
OF BLACK MEN

BLACK MEN
L♥VE

KENNETH WILSON

First Printing: 2022

ISBN: 979-8-9860894-3-0

Ordering Information:

Special discounts are available on quantity purchases by corporations, associations, educators, and others. For details, contact the publisher at the email listed below.

U.S. trade bookstores and wholesalers:
Please contact: info@businessofbooksmastermind.com.

DEDICATION

This book is dedicated to my Grandparents Robert and Willie Ruth Robinson. They were my first example of a healthy, loving relationship.

I hope I have made you both proud.

TABLE OF CONTENTS

LIST OF AUTHORS IN CHAPTER ORDER

1. David Khasar
2. Chip Baker
3. Adrian Taylor
4. Derrick L. Pearson
5. Dashward Jappah
6. Kenneth Robert Wilson
7. Charles Woods
8. Jordan W. Adams
9. Ryan H. Dunston
10. Nailah "Sunnie" Jones
11. Daniel McMaster
12. Joseph Henry
13. Sergio Vibetrill
14. Robert Tyree

BUT HEY, THAT'S JUST ME
David Khasar

If you're like me, you have a complicated relationship with love. At the same time, I wouldn't be where I am today without it. The way I interact with people is because of love. I never want to come off disrespectful or mean. I base my interactions on "the golden rule," treating others the way you want to be treated. Donald Glover, the comedian, writer, and artist, jokes about how adults have empathy. We don't go around punching people in the face because we wouldn't want somebody punching us in the face. We learn in elementary school this simple concept, but even adults forget this rule. Putting those things into practice for me is a big part of how I show love to strangers.

A big reason I act the way I do is because of love. There are ways to show strangers you love them in our day-to-day lives. Holding the door, paying for a meal, and letting people know when they have something in their teeth—are a few examples that come to mind. It's not hard to do, but hey, that's just me.

2

I'd like to think that I've experienced loving someone and truly being in love in my twenty-nine years of life. Falling in love with someone is one of the best feelings ever because we don't realize it until we're in the air and falling, like a skydive without a parachute. The thing that I never thought about was if I would be able to land after. I hope that if you're reading this, you get to experience it. Everything between you and your partner just clicks without either of you even trying. It's a beautiful feeling.

I'm not sure if you've noticed yet, but love can be a touchy subject for me. It's because I'm always second-guessing myself. People in my life have told me that it's too soon for me to be in love with someone. What I've realized is that love can be subjective. No two people, or more if that's your thing, fall in love the same way. That's just how I feel.

Now, I have some questions for you:

- How are you supposed to fall in love with someone?
- Is love-at-first-sight a real thing?
- Are "meet-cutes" the right way to meet someone?
- If your parents set you up on dates, is that the "right way" to meet someone?

Dating applications, work functions, mutual friends, if there's a right way to find a spouse or life partner, I obviously don't know how to do it. And the reason I say that is because people I love question my feelings towards those I've either been interested in or want to be friends with first. I know that I don't always make the best judgment of character, but I'll give you a chance until you give me a reason not to trust you.

Let me tell y'all about the first girl that I loved that loved me back. For the sake of privacy, I'm going to refer to her as "Blue." Blue and I met in elementary school. We didn't know each other and were in different social circles. It wasn't until seventh grade that we started noticing each other because we had some classes together and knew some of the same people. We got together around the end of eighth grade. We went to the eighth-grade grad dance together, and we would hang out all the time. She gave me my first kiss on our school trip before my promotion. Looking back at that memory, it was an innocent, sweet moment in my life. After that, we dated for two years, and it was literally puppy love.

To give you some insight about me, I'm extremely infatuated with music; it's my passion. And I'm always singing. For that, you could say it's because of my parents. Growing up, my parents were always singing around the house. My mom was part of a singing group in Nigeria with some of her family who would tour different churches in the country. My dad sings all the time around the house. He even does it while he's cooking. I sometimes think that my musical talent comes from him instead of my mom, but I know it's a healthy mixture of both of them. I'm pretty sure I get my musical taste from my older sister. I always hung around her while we were growing up. I learned a lot about music and other things from her, and I'm extremely grateful to her and my family for introducing me to my passion and embracing it as I grew up.

In the past few years, something that's become popular is "self-love." As I said earlier, I have a complicated relationship with love. Knowing I'm not the nicest person and I don't learn the same as everyone else makes it extremely difficult to love and appreciate what I do. I'm trying to learn how to forgive myself and be okay with making mistakes. I think that's a huge factor in loving yourself. Being one hundred percent unapologetically yourself is definitely a form of self-love. I'm still learning to love myself, but it's a process like everything in life. I'm in love with myself, and I still love what I do, and what I do is me.

ABOUT THE AUTHOR:

Social Media:

IG @dkhasar

FB @dkhasar

Email dkhasar@gmail.com

David K is a creative, born and raised in the San Francisco Bay Area. He graduated from the Academy of Art University, studying music production and sound design. His long-term goal is to change the world. He's able to start a conversation with anybody. He's currently the co-host of Community Coalition Show and Rhyme & Reason, which is a part of Black Squirrel Media Network.

LOVE IS INTERNAL, EXTERNAL, AND EVERLASTING
Chip Baker

"I am a product of a whole lot of people loving me."
Coach Donnie Jones

Love can be a tough, tricky thing to conquer. Certain aspects allow us to build and maintain love. It is important to know that love starts internally, spreads out externally, and lasts forever when we are intentional about it. I believe that there are three phases to loving the right way. Each phase requires work, but the work is worth it.

Love Yourself (Internal)

The first phase of love is to love yourself. Loving yourself is the most important and key foundation for love. It is not selfish to love yourself. When we love ourselves, we hold ourselves accountable for our actions. All of our thoughts, reflections, and actions are aligned because we love ourselves enough not to get

7

involved with things that are detrimental to us; this puts us on the right path while working to achieve our dreams. Loving ourselves gives us the freedom to be happy. It is a learned discipline by trial and error. Happiness comes from our daily disciplines of loving ourselves.

There have been times in my life that I have had to remind myself that I am worthy, I am enough, and that I was chosen and put in positions to do great things. When I had those doubts, I reminded myself that the Big Man made me how he wanted me to be, and he made me for a purpose. I just had to live out his will and do what I was supposed to do. If he brought me to it, I was not to doubt that he could take me through it. This journey of thinking positive thoughts and then aligning them with positive actions will help us learn to love ourselves.

We learn what we want and don't want in our life. We discover our negotiables and our non-negotiables. Wants can include our goals, dreams, aspirations, and systems for success. Our do not's may include toxic relationships, bad environments, and bad choices. Negotiables are things we are willing to adjust. Non-negotiables are things we are adamant about that we will not bend on. When we understand our wants, don't want, negotiable, and non-negotiables, it allows us to have balance in our life.

Balance = Love + Accountability

Balance is essential to loving ourselves. When we have balance, everything falls in line and flows smoothly. Balance comes from having an equal amount of love and accountability. If you love yourself too much and do not hold yourself accountable, you will make choices that leave you with regrets. If you have too much accountability, you will also have regrets and not feel as happy or fulfilled as you can be. The secret sauce—so you all hear it again—is loving ourselves and having balance lies in our ability to have equal parts of love and accountability in our life.

"Sometimes we get so caught up in thinking about what we DON'T have that we forget to be grateful for what we DO have."
Chip Baker

Gratitude is another component that helps in loving ourselves. We always need to remember that things could be better, but they could also be way worse. Therefore, we must be grateful for what we have and truly love that. When we love in that manner, it broadens our thoughts and love.

Once we master loving ourselves effectively, we then become equipped to go on and love others.

Love Others (External)

"We all need to be loved and feel that someone has our back."
Chip Baker

Loving others is the second phase of love. It is important to love others from a nonjudgmental lens, with pure-hearted intentions. We get what we give. Input equals output. What we put into something is what we will receive in return. Grace and forgiveness also must be in the recipe when we love others.

"Labels. You can't love somebody above the label you give them."
Miles McPherson

A nonjudgmental lens allows us not to put a label on someone. When we place labels on people, the level of love we can give them is limited. It is limited because placing a label gives them a cap on the amount of love that can be offered from us. Pure-hearted intentions show that we are giving love in a pure way and with no ill will. When the love given is pure, it is received as such and be returned in the same way.

Input = Output

This pureness allows us to get what we give. The input that we give equals the output from others that we receive. We can look at it like investments or a bank account. We must invest first to receive a return on our investment. In a bank account, we must make deposits first before we can make withdrawals. Love is the same way. When we love and invest in others, we receive the return from that investment. When we deposit pure love into others, we can make those withdrawals when we need them. But also, people will give love to us even when we do not realize that we need it. That is when love becomes magical!

I can recall several times in my life when people around me loved me. Regardless of my flaws, whether I thought I was worthy or not, and whether I gave it to them, they just loved me. To know that I had people like that around me made me feel special; this is why I encourage loving others, regardless.

None of us are perfect; we all make mistakes. Therefore, it is important to give grace and forgiveness. When we love the perfect imperfections in others, it sets us up for maximum growth together in our relationships. The beauty of loving others in that manner is that it sets us up for an exciting journey in the life of living and learning. Communication is heightened, respect is given, and trust is built, established, and maintained.

Loving others sets up a space for our loved ones to be loved. When we love others with our all, it creates an everlasting ripple effect. Our loved ones receive the benefit from the love we have given long after we are gone. Both sides of my family are made up of people that love others in a huge way. I can say that I have benefited and received love from people because my family members have loved them. People have had my back and looked out for me because my mother or father invested time, effort, or sewed positive encouragement into them. Both my parents have passed. It amazes me how people light up when they tell me stories about them.

I am also grateful that I have seen several instances where people have cared for younger people in my family because I have loved them. It is a great feeling to know that others will take care of your loved ones because you loved them. It encourages me to continue to be intentional about loving others.

"Love others; it is worth it!" ~ Chip Baker

Love What You Do (Everlasting)

"Sight is a function of the eyes, but vision is a function of the heart."
Myles Munroe

The third phase of love is loving what you do. It is important to love what we do; this creates a lasting love effect for those we have come in contact with in our lives. Our environments become infectious and contagious with spreading love. Loving what we do allows us to dig deep and have some substance about us. Loving what we do also allows us to grow through any challenges effectively.

It is beautiful to be in an environment where we can see our love infecting people the right way. Everything around becomes better. It spreads and becomes contagious. From there, love is the expectation. Anything less than that is not accepted. It all starts with you just loving what you do. It then goes on to make a lasting impact on the world.

Surface vs Substance

When we love what we do, it gives us substance. Substance is a word that means "a solid presence." When we have substance, all things are quality, all things have meaning, and all things have value. Things are not surface level when we have substance and love what we do.

"Love is life, and life is love."
Chip Baker

When we love ourselves, love others, and love what we do, we become love. It puts us in alignment with our assignment. Everything around us becomes great because we choose to love in a major way. Loving in the moment and being intentional about our love allows us to impact people we don't even know.

Love is the fundamental core root of everything great. God is love, we are love, and all greatness is love. Love comes in many shapes, sizes, colors, heights, widths, and above and beyond. Love is the basis of our being. Everything around us is instantly better when we love, let ourselves be loved, and give love. Environments of love allow for growth, success, failures, learning lessons from failures, and endless opportunities for exciting things to happen.

There are three phases of love. The first is Love Yourself. Loving yourself is internal. The second phase is Love Others. Loving others is external. The last phase is Love What You Do.

Loving what you do is everlasting. It creates a ripple effect that lasts forever. Love is Life Ongoing Vivaciously and Encompassing all.

May God bless you on your journey of LOVE!

Love is

L- Life

O- Ongoing

V- Vivaciously and

E- Encomposing all

ABOUT THE AUTHOR:

Social Media:

IG @chipbakertsc

FB @chipbakertsc

Email chipbakertsc@gmail.com

Chip Baker is a fourth-generation educator and has been a teacher/coach for over twenty-two years. He is a multiple-time best-selling Author, Youtuber/Podcaster, Motivational Speaker and Life Coach.

Chip Baker is the creator of the youtube channel/podcast "Chip Baker - The Success Chronicles," where he interviews people of all walks of life and shares their stories for positive inspiration and motivation.

Live. Learn. Serve. Inspire. Go get it!

Chip Baker Books

Growing Through Your Go Through

Effective Conversation to Ignite Relationships

Suited For Success Vol. 2

The Formula Chart for Life

The Impact of Influence

R.O.C.K. Solid

The Impact of Influence Vol. 2

Kids Book- Stay On The Right P.A.T.H.

The Impact of Influence Vol. 3

ROCKY ROAD

Adrian Taylor

I'm not easy to love. Honestly, if I were my partner, I would've run away the moment we locked eyes. Love can be a learning experience rather than just being a feeling. Yeah, it does feel good, sometimes bad, but once we get it right, it's a beautiful thing. I thank God for teaching me how to love and how to be loved. It's for sure more than its four letters. I thought I knew what love was as a teenager. Years and a few relationships later, I realized I wasn't in love at all, and neither were the girls I encountered. It was LUST. How the hell would a fourteen or fifteen-year-old kid think they're in love? Bust a nut and fall in the matrix. In reality, most folks have had this experience. But when you know, you know, right? When we get a real understanding of love, we will go to unthinkable measures to feel the love from that person we've slowly grown attached to over time. Some people will respect the growth and maturity, while others may not. This was us, breaking a few barriers.

My partner and I met in July of 2000 when I was running a little wild. I was just getting out of the county jail, and we clicked almost immediately. We never intended on falling in love. Although I had been in a few relationships in the past, none would compare to her. We were in for the ride of our lives, not knowing what the future would hold us. We grew closer and closer each day. We enjoyed the time we spent together. I've always been a believer in eyes; I believe they tell stories. I knew her story was nothing similar to mine, so I thought there was no way that would work, but every time I looked into her eyes, I would smile inside. I had no clue this was me feeling something for her, this was love, but I didn't know. Early in our relationship, I began to recognize how good of a heart this girl had, and I told myself that I needed to protect her, not only from tricks and games that went on in my world at the time but in the world in general.

In 2001 she showed me a sign of loyalty. We got arrested and went to jail together. I tried to take responsibility for everything we possessed, but she wouldn't let it go that way. Although we were evenly guilty, and I had been through this before, she hadn't, so I tried to protect her. I was already on thin ice with the judicial system, and she knew my circumstances at the time. She tried to protect me, and both our asses went to jail. I was mad at her, but I knew she did this from the heart. A few months later, I returned the favor. I wouldn't let it happen again, so I put her goods in my pocket when she got pulled over the next time. She was there outside the county jail, waiting for me thirty days later. This was love, and we had been through a few obstacles and managed to pull through them together, but this wouldn't be a fairytale, not now at least.

We had our share of little problems like any other couple, but we'd make amends between St. Ides, Steel Reserves, and Strange Clouds. She was more than my lover at this point; she was my best friend. Then, in August of 2003, we were blessed with a beautiful baby girl, Savanah; this was a life-changer for me. I finally had a purpose for living. Savanah was a brand new love like none other. I knew I'd always love her mother the minute she birthed her. It was then that I gave her my heart forever, in full. Now we were really able to come out of any other shells that we may have held back. Making the baby smile made her mother smile, so I let out a silly side of myself that only my mother and little brother had ever witnessed, just to see them both smile. Two years later, God gave us another blessing in the form of a prince, Joshua. He had ocean blue eyes. This little guy made my heart beat differently, with another purpose to be a better man. He loved when I'd act stupid, throwing myself on the floor as if being knocked out by his tiny fists. That little laugh was priceless. I loved it and loved him.

Little did I know, life was about to get very toxic for us, in the form of human beings and alcohol. It pulled us apart, and we went our separate ways. For a while, we both kept ourselves around the worst company. It was a true test. I would pray about things for both of us, and I let it run its course. The reality was that we were young and misdirected. I was in a constant state of drunkenness and random flings, and she was in the company of her biggest hater. Blinded, poisoned by the words of her enemy's persuasion, she was coerced into doing the same things as me. It was all bogus on both our part, but one thing that was for sure was that we loved each other deeply by now. God had to be laughing while he let this thing play out. Crazy asses.

Love is more of a learning experience rather than just being a feeling. Yeah, it does feel good. Sometimes bad, but we slowly learn the things that trigger these emotions. When I met my partner, we weren't in a state of love; love takes time. And we did time, so to speak. Some relationships are meant to be great with no bumps, while some are spades for hearts. Only God knew our plan...

November 21, 2007

I made the mistake of getting tangled up in something I had no damn business even being around; a quick drunken thought turned into a bunch of trumped-up charges—another bogus moment. The next day it all hit me ... I had two kids, and I'm in jail. These folks were talking about ten years. I knew I was better than what I had gotten myself into this time. The situation was fucked up, and the only people I had in my corner were my mom and my brother Jermaine. All I could think about was my kids, though, and it hurt me to my heart. Everything was wrong and all my fault if I had to go up the road. That would be the last drunken mistake I would make. I prayed on it all. By this time, Savanah was four years old, and Joshua was two. I had to get myself out of this jam. While waiting on my fate in the jail, a third blessing came, and my second daughter, Shamiya, joined the world.

I had to get the fuck out of there and quick. And as fate would have it, in February of 2008, I was lying in the cell reading when a guard came in with a clipboard. After he made sure I was the right person, I was told to pack my shit; I was going home. I had no clue how this happened, but somebody bailed me out. It was my love. She got me out just so I could meet Shamiya, which she didn't birth. That was real love, and we started a new chapter. We were going to do it right this time. We knew I was going back. I knew that if I got through this, I'd need to make big changes for the people and things that really mattered. While I was out, we worked on a new us. We got that communication back. We showed one another as much love and affection as we could with the time we had before I had to go to face the judge. I went back to court in the middle of that April. For the drunken mistake, I was sentenced to ten years. They suspended all but three. She was there for me the whole time, still showing me love. While it would be another obstacle to conquer, we did it! She stayed faithful and took care of our children and apartment. I told myself that I needed to return the love and show as much appreciation as much as I could when I got out. At the end of May 2009, I was released. Who was there when I walked out of the jail's front door? My love.

By March of 2010, baby Avah came into the world. It was then that we both realized that this was just right. We'd gone through the bad in order to get to the good. We weren't perfect, and we understood that. We got married the following year. God's plan. If there is something or someone you love that makes you the best man you can be, love them unconditionally. No one is perfect in life.

Learn from your mistakes together, and do what it takes to achieve the happiness that was meant for you. It's worth fighting for more than anything. Your higher power will put all thing's into place. For us, the blueprint was laid out from the beginning; we just didn't know how to follow it. We had to knock the old building down, and rebuild a new one, AS ONE.

Then on August 17, 2020, I found that I had stage 4 throat cancer. It rocked my world, our world. We were in a beautiful groove, and now this. I never panicked in life or love before, and I wouldn't now. We went into battle mode. She was there with me at every appointment. This shit was life-changing, and I worried about my kids. I had a huge decision to make now: take a risk and go with the easier route with less pain and life adjustments that may only give men a few extra years to live or live another twenty-plus year. I chose the latter. It was love that made me do the right thing. On my father's birthday, September 28, 2020, she was the last person I saw before I went under, and she was there with my mother when I opened my eyes. I am now in remission, and she's still there. WE'RE STILL HERE!

I look at love a lot differently these days. Sometimes we fall in love before we really know what it is. We went through the time and struggles that would've kept most couples separated permanently. It's important to learn about each other along the way, and that will lead to a healthy bond that won't be broken. We cracked the code to happiness by going through the pain that we endured together. Twenty years later, she's still by my side, and I won't leave hers.

When she birthed my first child, I felt something for her that I had never felt before. I know now that that feeling was love.

   We're Bonnie and Clyde, although different. The love we share is one. That's my "appa scrappa." We smile together. Every day isn't perfect, but we cherish them. Respect your partner. That is love, the way it's supposed to be. You got my front, and I got your back. Really that's how it always was, and we just had to see it.

ABOUT THE AUTHOR:

Social Media:

IG @taylorpride6

FB @adrian.taylor.7547

Email taylorprideempire@gmail.com

Adrian Taylor was born in Olney, Maryland, and raised in Silver Spring, Maryland. He was raised by a single mother which helped him develop strong moral grounds for love, loyalty, and respect. He is a father of five amazing children, Savanah, Joshua, Symone, Shamiya, and Avah. Every day Adrian is looking to make himself smarter, stronger, and better than he was yesterday. He wrote this in hopes of helping others realize that sometimes love doesn't fit into society's perfect story or definition. It can be a hard rocky road. Love, like most of us, is not perfect.

WHAT IS BLACK MALE LOVE? (TO ME)

Derrick L. Pearson

What is love? What is black? What is a man? What is Black Man Love?

I was asked to define and express Black Man Love and add how I define the topic in a way that seems fair and truthful. I would never try to define it for others. I am just learning what it means to me, and the meaning changes daily. Various times, locations, and elevations require redefining and refining, so I will sit quietly and reach into my heart to tell you what these things mean to me now, as I am, from where I was at the time.

Love is the highest ambition. Love is the greatest thing we can do and be at any time or place. It elevates and enhances, and it removes its opposite to exist. Love cannot exist where hate or fear does. It will not live where hate or fear does. Read that again. Love is forward from where you are, be it alone or coupled. Alone is the love of self. Coupled is of another. Love coupled requires true love alone. Love requires knowledge and understanding of self. It allows knowledge and love of another. Love must be active in both. It cannot be absent in either. This is my definition of love.

Next is the Black. It describes internal strength with external expression. Black is beautiful and powerful. Black is dominant in science and is the description attached to its reaction to the sun and the universe. Black can be brown, tan, or pale, depending on the location of its person, and has been misidentified enough to bastardize its actual meaning. Black is not evil or despair. Let's agree that Black is a genetic marker and a cultural phenomenon for this chapter. It is a historical storyteller and an intriguing mystery within our humanity. Being Black is a core value of expression, activity, culture, and pride. It is beautiful, powerful, and me.

A man can be identified/defined as a gender, sex, or being. It can define some of us, all of us, and the spirit of how we engage at any time. It can define an adult male, person, or servant. It can be confused with male and has been used to lessen others in deeming them less than a man or two-thirds a man.

What is Black Man Love?

Black Man Love, by my definition, is the highest level of human love I have lived in my life. It is the conscientious decision to act in my greatest caring for myself or another; simply stated, love is a purposeful decision. It is being the most worthwhile of humans, for myself and others. In addition, it is the standard for which I live and love, daily and forever forward. Black man love is being proud to love no matter anyone else's feeling about who I love (including myself) and how I love, and what love means to them rather than what it means to me and us. Black Man Love is respectful of self, another, and others, all because it has been deemed as such. Black Man Love understands its power, its threat, and its responsibility.

Here is want I want to do with this:

I grew up in a home filled with love. (I call it a home because love lived there. Houses do not always contain love; homes do.) The home may or may not have had traditional love. There was not always a man in it to help me know what that kind of love should/would look like consistently. I will highlight that statement. "should/would look like" I will come back to that later. My mother was not always with someone, so I saw single mom love. That "tougher than need be love" because two-sided and united love was not possible at times. That "we are family like on TV love" where mom and dad held it down and directed their kids to grow up and love like they do. I saw and experienced a "get through" kind of love. A "this will do until real love shows up" kind of love. I did not need anything else because we only covet what we see and know from people we look like and know. Every other kind of love was for someone else because I knew it did not look like me.

I did not know my biological father. The man that I thought was my father and who gave me the last name Pearson was not my father. He also was not around me long enough to make a positive impact on how I loved or lived. I do not really know him, and I am not really bothered by his absence. Love chooses. I would have loved him regardless had I been allowed the opportunity. There was stepdad

Jack, and he did his best to love in the way he knew, which was not really love at all. He tried to love in ways he knew were better for us, but he was not capable. Finally, there was my stepdad Roland who I called "Pops" because he earned it. He cared. He showed up and stayed present. He taught. He loved. He was flawed, but we all are. I was simply happy to get some of the love I wanted, even if it was not all I wanted. I learned that love was not perfect. No love is perfect. Real love is close. Authentic love is close.

Black man love is an accumulation of the love you see, the love you seek, and the bridges and barriers you cross and deal with along the way. I am well-traveled in the seeking of love. I just took a while to figure out what love should be rather than should not. You know what love is, to give it and share it. Love of self. Love of another. Love together. I had to relearn love.

I am the product of a Black community, and it's surrounding white and blended communities. My neighborhood was Black. My school was Black. My friends were Black. And then, busing happened. I was plucked from my Black world and placed in the middle of white communities, schools, people, and activities. I had to relearn everything. I had to find and create friends. I had to learn different music, dress codes, and diets. I had to learn about new television shows and movies. I had to see everything as one thing. Mine.

In those schools, I had to determine what should be my interests and intentions. I had to figure out who I could trust and who I should not trust. I had to be cautious of dark corners and white faces, and I had to find peace in the middle. I was judged for leaving my neighborhood to find friends and favorites. I was judged for going home when I was done. I was seeking love. Love of self, other, and together.

I recall hanging out with some friends in the neighborhood and having a mom whisper to one of my (girl)friends, "I hope you aren't thinking about dating him, girl. You might be related." I was young, and it resonated heavily without knowing what it meant. I got sent home. I asked my mother what the woman meant and got a shoulder shrug. It happened again, same words, different house. I asked why. It seemed to be common, or just how it was. Love in my neighborhood had secrets. Some of it was shame. Some were just labeled as "it was what it was." As I reached the dating years, I figured out how not to deal with it. Date girls who were not my relatives. Or color. Or from my neighborhood.

I soon realized that the conversations between mothers and daughters changed when I went love fishing in a different pool or pond. Some parents did not want my love for their daughters for distinct reasons. They did not want it for them because I was Black. I found myself seeking parents' and daughters' love and wanted them to love me for me. I wanted them to love me because I was good, and I wanted to be loved by their daughters because I was good. It should not have to be that hard.

I found love in the most unusual places—like on a date with someone else. We would go to the beach and party at the end of the school year. One year, the house next to us was filled with girls from our neighboring county. They went to a rival school, and that helped bridge the gap as we were miles away from home for a week. I became intrigued by a young lady, and we spent the week together. We promised not to be a summer fling and agreed to hang out when we were back home. She called (yes, kids, an actual phone call on a landline phone attached to the wall) and invited me to a party at a friend's house. I was supposed to bring my friends to meet her's, and the party would be great. In those days, house parties included music and dancing, usually in the living room. I danced with my date and could not help noticing this adorable blonde staring at me dancing. I asked my date who she was and was told that she was the host. It was her party. I paused for a minute and told my date I needed to meet her. I left the dance floor and introduced myself. I asked her to dance, and she said no. "I don't dance like you do." Ouch. I said I would show her. Instead, we talked until the morning hours, talking about ourselves and each other. I met her parents soon after, and we all talked. They liked me. I liked them. I liked her. Like became love. Authentic love. Her name was Beckie.

Remember the learning to love thing? Beckie and I knew early on that we wanted to grow old together. No matter who came along, it was going to be us in the end. Apparently, after years together, my girl grew into a lady and proposed the idea of marriage. I did not say she proposed, she proposed the idea, and I totally missed the proposal. We floated in different directions, getting together whenever for whatever reason, but somehow never crossing the line to being together forever. She married, I married, but not to each other. I failed in learning to love and how to be loved. Decades later, we crossed paths on social media. It only took a few messages before a phone call, and that phone call led to old connections and feelings.

We had grown up. We had changed. But in those changes, there was still love.

Beckie was living in Virginia, and I was in Utah. We decided to meet up, and I am positive that it took us five minutes to know that we would be together. Truth. We did a quick check on our current relationships and moved forward. We would move in together in Virginia, and I would get to work on setting my career path to D.C. Whatever version of us existed, it was enough to move forward with forever as the GPS. The love was strong enough to make it work. The home would be love-filled enough to make it work.

Full disclosure, I had never had to disclose my faults to anyone fully. I never had to bear my weaknesses to anyone fully. Getting together decades later required several bridges to be disclosed. Declaring personal flaws, learning to trust the truth, my truth, putting down childish behaviors, and choosing to focus on love rather than not was a constant classroom in the home. Sharing your greatest flaw with someone is difficult, especially when that person matters the most. I had to learn that the greatest gift of love I could give her was to share that with her. I had to let her know my flaws. I had to learn to accept hers. We had to learn to accept and love each other, flaws and all. We were better once everything was exposed, discussed, and known. That is a gift that we can give to you all. Trust. Those flaws can be weights that drown you or vessels to move you forward. Choose forward.

The most difficult days and nights of my marriage were those where entire truths and absolute flaws were shared. Baring your soul

30

to the person who means the most to you is frightening. Learning that they love you anyway is the greatest evidence of actual love possible. She not only needed to know my truths and flaws, but I also needed to know hers. We had to know each other at our best and worst in order to exist at our best. Mandatory. You both deserve it. You both require it.

Beckie helped me focus, she demanded my best, and I celebrate her for it. I am better with her, because of her, for her. The same is true with her. We hold each other up, accountable, and high. I thought I knew love, Black Man Love, as a life of prowess, power, and persuasion. I had to unlearn that. I needed to accept Black Man Love as truth, faith, and home. I had to accept that I was worthy of love, from myself, from her, from us. She was worthy of love from herself, me, and us. It was there that the power of truth and home blossomed and elevated us both. A home deserves no enemies or foes within. That is what makes a home special. Home is where Black Man Love shines, prospers, and matures.

I love better, greater, and more completely now. I trust more, believe more, and praise more. I rely on my love, call on her, and move with her. That is this kind of love. Purposeful. Directed. Honest. Connected.

Understanding American Black Man Love requires an understanding of self. Your location. Your history. Your geography. Your DNA. Your faith. Your heart. Your home.

Black Man Love is the ability to love yourself when others do not or won't.

It is faith in something greater than you, us, for you and us.

Black Man Love is the choice to choose home over house.

It is the accountability for flaws and the value of truth.

Love is finding another to love, and you should love yourself.

It is finding the love of yourself, the best love of yourself, for another.

Black Man Love is being active in love, being honest in love, and any two people being united in love.

Being strong when asked to be weak. Finding beauty in your different skin. Back straight when asked to kneel. Chest out being proud when being strapped across the back. Looking eye to eye when being asked to lower them. Being better than when considered less than. Accepting seventy-four percent pay for one-hundred percent of the work. Being whole when considered two-thirds a man.

To me, Black Man Love is being above the petty, beyond the judgment, and at home wherever he is, whenever he is; however, he believes in a greater, crafting peace at home, knowing the value of love no matter what.

That is Black Man Love. Faith. Home. Truth.

To me.

ABOUT THE AUTHOR:

Social Media:

IG @derrickpearson

FB @derrick.pearson.5

Email pearsonderrick@aol.com

Derrick Pearson is a Radio Co-Host of "The DP and Stephens Show" at 93.7 the Ticket FM in Lincoln, Nebraska. He was also a speaker at TEDxLander in May of 2019: The Love Project and a speaker at TEDxDeerPark in March of 2020: An American Face.

Derrick "DP" Pearson brings his unique brand of energy to The Ticket's midday, "The DP and Stephens Show." DP has spent time during his career as a sportscaster, radio and television host, writer, manager, and high school coach. That career has taken him nationwide, including Washington, DC, Charlotte, Los Angeles, Salt Lake City, and Atlanta. In addition to his media and coaching ventures. He also helped establish Fat Guy Charities in Charlotte, an NFL Charity, and developed LovePrints, a national mentor program that promotes loving and learning through sports. DP joins Tom Stephens every weekday from 11 a.m. to 2 p.m.

I KNOW ME BETTER THAN YOU THINK

Dashward Jappah

Love is not an action, but it's a series of choices to act. It is the decision you make when you don't feel like it, but the sheer will you have and commitment will not let you fall and become someone who is not dependable. Love is choosing to keep a fifth child after losing your job, not knowing how you will feed an extra mouth, but knowing he will be fed. It sounds immature, but your faith and work ethic must be different. Love is surprising your son with a graduation gift years later because when he graduated from high school, the family was living in a hotel and could not afford to gift him at that moment. It is giving your brother a guide on how he can run his business properly after he just crashed your car and your monthly payment went up. I do not think love is about resiliency, but I know it is not about being perfect. It's about choosing to forgive and choosing to heal those wounds from the past so the scars cannot transcend through other generations.

My family has its things like most families. Everyone, including myself, is not the best at communication. We have all jumped to conclusions, used unfair angles in arguments, and have been impatient. However, even in the worst situations, I have never felt neglected by my family. I may have felt misunderstood at times, but I know I can be more understanding. Often, we can become blind to our actions when focusing on the behaviors of others. But I grew up. When I have something to say, I say it, just as when someone has something to say to me, I listen. Not everything is about right or wrong. Sometimes just addressing what an issue is can help you diffuse a situation. But once again, it is a choice if you want to work it out. That is love.

Now, as I have gotten older, I have always wanted to share this love with others. It does not always mean kissing, sex, or dates. But for me, it is the feeling of being comfortable, welcomed, listened to, and not judged. I wanted to be on a sports team and have guys I am not related to feel like family. We never could afford sports, so what I saw on TV was the closest thing I knew to it. I just thought the idea of being overlooked by people and being underdogs and then coming back to win the championship would make my life completely different. To go into detail about most of the sports I played, the camaraderie we had on those teams would be overkill. Long story short, I fell in love with the idea of what a team should be. I do not hate any old teammate, but I cannot genuinely say I felt like a brotherhood playing high school sports, and as I have gotten older, I am really okay with that. I did not have too much in common with people. I was quiet. Some teammates talked about others and the truth of how the industry was just as money-hungry and politic as others were starting to dawn on me. Safe to say, my biggest mind shift happened after turning seventeen.

At twenty-three years old, sometimes the one thing I can think about when I work out or play basketball or football is how stupid and underwhelming most of my coaches were at their jobs. I never hated any of my teammates even though we were never really the best of friends, and as we got older, we did get closer, but the lack of chemistry and cooperation as a team was more due to the disfunction of coaches. It became a joke to us just how we saw them running plays from last week that did not work and how quick they were to jump on players' necks about something they told us to do. Of course, we did not say anything. We were basically kids, and in all honesty, "my coach doesn't like me" has been manipulated into you're lazy, just try harder. No one thinks to ask when a little Black boy's mental well-being is at stake. I guess they have it all figured out.

I have linked back with a few of those guys I played sports with as I have gotten older. We do not always talk football, but instead, we ask about each other's health, families, and life goals. I even train one of my old teammates and have supported the clothing lines of some friends. My best friend Leandra, who I have known since I was fifteen and was a trainer on the football team, is still someone I talk to regularly. She cooks, does nails and lashes, the whole nine yards. I never got to run into the middle of the field and held a trophy with my teammates and coaches, nor had Nick Saban, one of the most established college coaches, walked through my door and given me an offer. But I realized I was looking for an artificial idea of love. I realized God wanted me to look at those supporting me now, and sports were my gateway towards feeling that love from those years prior. Of course, I wish I had better coaches, but more importantly, I hope they didn't make me feel the way I did when I played for them: useless, weak, gaslighted, and dismissed. All I can think about as I get closer to becoming a coach is that I never want any player to feel that way. I know everyone cannot be saved, but that does not mean everyone should not get the same opportunity to get shown love. You never know who you could have helped just by being gentle with someone. You could be the reason why a kid wants to open homeless shelters or coach other kids when they get older. So, my choice now is to make an impact and make any child I come in contact with feel heard and cared for every day.

Now I understand the meaning of love a lot more. So how can I have all this knowledge of love without not one successful relationship with a woman that is not a relative or a friend? The thing is, it is very simple. It is a choice. I have never cheated or been physically or emotionally abusive to past partners, but there are plenty of unsuccessful relationships where neither party acted in such a way. So, what is it? I have met girls, went on dates, enjoyed each other's presence for two to three months, and then the relationship hit a ceiling. " I did not communicate as well with this girl. I'll get better at that for the next one," or "I did not realize I was being dismissive. I will try better with the next one." I would tell myself. I thought I was taking accountability. "You treat them too nice, too early on. Do not break your everyday routine for them.

Take it slow. I know you want to share your love, but a lot of people may not be ready for that," a coworker told me. I took the last one slowly, and the pattern repeated. I met a lovely young lady, and she told me about her past relationships. I didn't want to be like her exes. I got the things she mentioned. To surprise her, listen to her issues, and stroke her back when she puts her head on my shoulder. We had conversations about why we are not official yet, why she has not met my parents, or why we have not moved in together yet. And I was always right not to give in. Why? Wait for it, "You're really sweet. I just do not think I am ready for a relationship," or "This is really hard for me to do, but I do not see this becoming long term," or my favorite, "I just think we would be better off as friends." Most were through a text, but I did have one girl who was gracious enough to send a voice note. It is okay to laugh at that, I promise.

I guess I don't understand love. I thought I had learned from past relationships, but I guess I am not the catch I thought I was. In all honesty, if they wanted me around, they would try to keep me around instead of avoiding conversations that could've saved a relationship. I never lied to myself by saying, "I'm too nice." That will never be enough for any relationship, so do not fool yourself either. I was confused until I realized I had not loved myself as much as I could. I wouldn't eat as much and stopped working out. I'd go ghost from posting about my business online, and yes, I know how pitiful, just for a girl. But this goes back to me falling in love with love. I fell in love with TV's idea of love so much. I would look at how my family lived and be sad we could not always go on trips and do the stuff other families had the money to do, even if I did not always show it. I thought high school sports was the end and be-all, and I will never be a successful athlete with a great team.

But through all of that, I came to understand through those interactions, -the people I still talk to today, bring me food when I did not ask, support my business, and listen to me vent; those people chose to do all of that do it out of love. I know it hurts. To show love to someone who made it seem like they showed interest, but you don't want to love someone who does not love you. Maybe all those girls were right to break up with me. It wasn't that I was a terrible partner or that we were better off as friends, but I was not following the path God wanted, and it did not include any of those women. I felt a lot better when I was by myself, working out, going to weekly bible studies, not going to parties, smoking weed, drinking, and always trying to be someone's boyfriend. I was the best me and felt happiest when I was doing things to help myself so that I could help others. That self-love beats all.

You love yourself more, and you start being real with yourself. Something I would not like to talk about at that age of around fifteen that I don't care about now is my sensitivity. I saw it as a weakness until I realized just how much people will take it for granted. A lot of time, the more sensitive you are about your life decisions, the more militant you would want to move. You want to take your steps more carefully, but that doesn't mean you will be walking up steps forever. You will meet your destination when the time is right. If you force it, you will be humbled. If you're too hesitant, you start to lose faith in your ability. Thinking about my sensitivity makes me feel closer to God in a sense. You understand energy and when someone or something is off. You recognize when someone's feelings are not being catered to, and you also realize how best to get through to people. Often, cry baby is a shame tactic for "why do you care so much when I don't." Shame tactics are a weird way of policing emotions people do not want to validate. But there is true power in vulnerability. And the thing is, we come into this world crying. That must be the most human reaction possible. It is okay to cry, just have some tissues and a plan so you do not keep walking into those situations, and do not fret over what is not in your control.

I feel we give too much power to the Devil sometimes when it is really God blessing us. He is removing those you showed love to from your life because they are not supposed to be a part of your story. It is okay to be wrong, cry, and show emotion, but it is not okay to project and not communicate, as that is a form of self-sabotage. Be picky with who you communicate with and about what. And always remember your life plan before you make a decision and trust the process. If I officially made some of those girls mine, moved in with them, or did not believe in my family and decided to rebel, love would not be what I am writing about today. I can honestly say I could cry tears of joy more for the man I am becoming than I could tears of sorrow for the low self-esteem kid I was when I was fourteen. I think that was part of the plan and love God had for me. And I am choosing to love this plan more and more every day. I am not fully healed but trust me, I know myself better than you, who have yet to experience me, think I do.

ABOUT THE AUTHOR:

Social Media:

IG @jappahtunity

FB @dashward.jappah

Email edjappah5@gmail.com

Dashward Jappah is a twenty-three-year-old who was born in Fort Worth, Texas. He has lived around Atlanta for the longest and is a writer and personal trainer. In addition, Dashwand owns DashFix Services LLC. His goal is to help people understand that health is as generational as wealth. He believes that your kids do not do what you say but what you do. Also, You can definitely enjoy life reach fitness goals, and eat what you like at the same time, do not let that TV fool you.

Dashwand is a first-generation American. His parents are Liberian. He is very rooted in his ancestry and proud of where he came from.

Something Dashwand plans on doing with my best friends is starting a youth sports club. They played football together and wanted to start with football and track and field. Personally, Dashwand loves these sports, but I also can remember how unrewarding his experience was when he played. He does not want only to help kids get into college but wants them to be successful in the world mentally and emotionally. Dashwand wants to be the coach players still talk about when they have kids. For those adolescents ages fourteen to twenty, he is building his program for you. Having emotions and not really understanding them is normal. And you are not alone.

I KNEW I FOUND THE ONE

Kenneth Robert Wilson

My wife and I had been friends long before we got married. We met in middle school and started dating off and on in high school. By the time college came around, we were in a full-blown courtship. By this point in our relationship, we had become very close and knew a lot about each other. We came from two very different backgrounds and cultures. Her family is from Trinidad and Tobago, and mine is African American. She also came from a very large, close-knit family and was raised by both parents in a very loving Christian household.

My family was different. My father left when I was young. Though I knew who he was, we didn't have a real relationship. He would visit sometimes, but those visits rarely ended on a good note. He would argue and fight with my mom, at times being violent. He would often make false promises to me, including buying me a fire truck. When I was really young, I believed him. I wanted that fire

43

truck so bad! I would have dreams of playing with that toy. Whenever we were out, I would point at real fire trucks. Every time he would call and tell me he was bringing the fire truck, I would get so excited. Then he would show up … and he would never bring the fire truck. I would get so upset, and he would make excuses and promise he would bring it the next time he came. The next time would come, and he still wouldn't have the fire truck as promised. As time went on, his visits became fewer and fewer. My expectations diminished, and my hope turned into frustration and anger. By the time I became a teenager, I didn't see much of my father. The dream of a fire truck was long gone. It became part of a sour and almost hateful memory of a man that wasn't there for me and never delivered on his promises. It hurt me, and I carried that hurt and anger into my adulthood.

During our time of courtship, while we were still in college, I would often tell my wife stories of my childhood. I felt it was important that she knew and understood my family history and dynamics, as it was very different from hers. It was not easy for me to do, and, in fact, I would be terrified before I told her. Some of the stories were extremely traumatic for me, and I wasn't sure how she was going to take them. They were stories that I had never told anyone before her, and she will be the only person that will ever hear some of those stories. One of the stories I told her was about the fire truck. I told her how my dad would promise and promise to buy me a fire truck and never deliver. Now for me, this wasn't one of the more terrifying stories I told her, but it was one of the more impactful. It brought up a lot of emotion for me to even talk about it. I remember almost crying and really feeling angry the first time I told her. At the time, I was embarrassed because I was so emotional (also part of my trauma). As always, she was very attentive and would ask me questions. My baby would always make me feel comfortable sharing some of these intense and intimate parts of my life. I knew that I could confide in her, and she could do the same with me. There was no one I trusted more. It was a big part of why our bond became so strong.

One Christmas, while we were still in courtship, we decided to spend time together and visit each other's families. I went to meet her and spend time with her family first. We had previously decided to exchange gifts, which was a big deal because we were still in our early twenties and broke. That year I don't remember what I brought her as a gift. I think it was a small necklace I found at the local Piercing Pagoda at the mall. It wasn't much, but it was all I could afford. I was still excited because just buying my baby a present was special to me. When it came time to exchange gifts, I gave her the necklace first. I could tell she liked it, but she was really excited to give me her present. I remember she had to go to another room to get it. There was a bit of suspense as I had to wait for her to come back. I was getting nervous because, at first, maybe she didn't like my gift after all. In reality, she was only gone for a couple of seconds, and she came back with a rectangular box. It was still in the brown shipping paper with the labels still on the paper. I was really curious and excited, but I had no idea what was in this box. I tried to play it cool and remove the shipping paper slowly to keep the paper intact (I'm glad I did). Once I removed the paper, I could finally see what it was. It was a brand new toy fire truck!

I think my heart skipped a beat as I finally recognized what it was. I have never been so surprised in my life. My face and my body were stuck, and I could not move. It took me a couple of seconds to process what was happening. Once my brain figured it out, then came the emotions. My eyes began to water, and I didn't even try to fight back the tears. It was a moment of pure joy for me. I immediately gave my baby a hug, which seemed like it lasted forever. The only words that would come out of my mouth were "thank you."

At the moment, I knew that this was an important event in my life, but it took some time to realize how immensely significant and life-changing this was for me. First, I finally got a fire truck. After my dad never brought me one, I never purchased one of my own. No one else had brought me one. As I got older, I thought my desire to own a fire truck went away. However, holding the physical truck in my hands brought back all the desires, anticipations, and joy I wanted to experience as a kid. It was like the six-year-old boy was back, and I could feel the emotions all over again. It didn't matter that I was now a young adult. All that mattered was that I finally had my fire truck.

As happy as I was to have my fire truck, I was most impacted by the love and actions of my girlfriend. As time goes on and the more I think about her actions and the gift, the more significant it becomes to me. For me, this was not a regular Christmas gift; this was a release of years of childhood trauma that had begun to spill over into my young adult years. I was able to acknowledge how hurt I had been and now let it all go. I knew that she had been listening and paying attention when I told her all of my childhood stories. From that, she was able to focus on the stories that were most important to me. She really put thought into researching and locating model fire trucks and took the time and money to purchase one (which are not cheap). Being a young college student at the time, I knew this was a big deal for her. I'm sure she even asked her parents and other family members for help. This gift took real compassion, time, effort, money, and thoughtfulness. It took years of building a genuine relationship through courtship and really learning and trying to understand everything we could about each other, good and bad. That was one of the first moments I can remember feeling the deeper layers and levels of love. It was a big part of our foundation, which later became our union in marriage. Learning and a deep understanding of each other are one of the true strengths of our relationship.

As for the fire truck … I still have it. It is still in the original shipping packaging and box. I rarely take it out. I do not play with it. No one plays with it. It is kept in a secret location far away from the curious and often destructive hands of my beautiful children. That fire truck is my physical evidence of true love.

ABOUT THE AUTHOR:

Please see lead author info in the About The Lead Author section at the end of the book.

HOW EASY IS IT TO LOVE

Charles Woods

I love you! It's amazing how these words can be so hard to say. They can also be used very loosely. When I say I love you, you better believe I mean it. These words do not come from me trying to sound tough. It comes from my heart.

I have never looked for someone to lead me or guide me. My love comes from me, from deep within. We live in a world where a large percentage of people are looking for approval: think about social media. The majority of people on social media do not have a personal connection with the individuals commenting on their page. For some reason, if there are not a thousand or more likes on a post, someone may not be considered relevant. The thing about it is, that negativity seems to get the most attention. What do likes on social media really mean? Why should these likes determine how you feel about yourself? What happened to the days when being a good person mattered? I am not the mythological Roman god, Cupid, or love expert, but I do know you have to love yourself before you can love anyone else.

As a Black man, I choose positivity and love. I do not have the time or make time for negativity and hate. This world is filled with too much of that already. I am grateful to wake up in the morning and know that I can surround myself with great people. It is my choice, and everyone has that same right and ability. Believe me. It wasn't easy creating this type of environment for myself, but it was a must, and I had to make sure it happened.

Who is Influencing You, or Are You the Influencer?

Why do you think the way you do? Why do you do the things you do? Are you being influenced by someone? Are you the influencer?

I have always been the captain of my soul. I have always had my own mind. There is one phrase that I remembered my mother saying when I was an adolescent. When she noticed that I had no problem with being by myself, she said, "I love that he can go in his room or the back yard and entertain himself. He doesn't need a crowd or anyone acknowledging him. He is self-motivated." Without a doubt, I have always been self-motivated. That comes with loving myself and all my imperfections. My surroundings could be in chaos, but that will not determine my life. I am grateful for every day that I open my eyes. I realized early on that I have the opportunity to make a difference with any and everything that pertains to me. I have that choice. I choose to smile and surround myself with positive and uplifting people. I have no time for negative individuals that thrive on tearing others down. I choose to love my life because I have been given the gift of life. I did not have to be here. Sulking about the things that I do not have or the situation I was given will never make things better. No sir! I am not going to miss out on any types of opportunities that are out there for me. I am not going to waste time being angry, upset, or filling my body with hate. I love myself too much. I love this opportunity of life too much.

Find a Reason to Love: I Love You Anyway

Going through life, I have experienced many positive reasons to love. I choose to focus on those reasons and continue to learn and grow. As an adolescent, our family dog would wait at the front door for my sister to come home at the front door and when her bus arrived, our dog would meet her at the bus stop to make sure she got home safely. As I got older, my sister would walk me to daycare and then walk herself back in the same direction as she made her way to school. As I got a little older, I would go to work with my father and his roofing crew. They taught me how to shingle a roof and earn my own money. I was learning the value of hard work. I made money for passing shingles to them as they tacked those shingles down. That ended up being a valuable time that I was able to spend with my father. There were also days that I should have been going to my afternoon kindergarten class, but I was either at work, fishing, or hunting with my father. School should have been the first priority, but as I got older, I realized I didn't have too many of those opportunities to spend that type of quality time with my father.

In elementary and middle school, teachers tried many different strategies to make sure I was getting the best-personalized education possible. Teachers continued to push me outside my comfort zone, only hoping to bring out the best in me. They placed me in upper-level classes, and I competed on academic teams. In junior high and high school, coaches saw things in me that I did not see. They ensured that I knew the game and was always prepared for competition. They trained me to be a leader in all my settings.

When I got to high school, I believed in treating people right, and I loved everyone. That does not mean that everyone is your friend. It means leading with kindness; it's okay if we don't agree. Our differences are what make us unique individuals, but we can respectfully disagree and peacefully function in the same environment. It was important for me to surround myself with a great group of friends that uplifted and supported each other. These gentlemen are considered my brothers, and we remain close to this day. Most of my friends lived in single-parent homes with mothers who were taking the lead in their children's lives. These wonderful mothers and great women took me in and treated me as their own. They literally took me in and let me stay in their homes. Words cannot explain how grateful I am for the love and support that I was shown by these phenomenal mothers.

I won homecoming king my senior year of high school, which meant a lot to me because this came from the student body, Class of 95! That year, my athletic ability gave me a chance to continue my education at an institution of higher learning, at no charge. Well, I guess it was no charge. Football was like having two jobs. The opportunities continued to grow, and I was named team captain my senior year in college; another distinction given to me by my peers. When I graduated, I was offered another opportunity to continue my education as a graduate assistant football coach through the football program. The program paid for me to obtain a master's degree. It was hard work, but not many individuals get this chance.

When I left Lafayette, I had two degrees and tons of experience, and I saw so many different places in the United States. It was life-changing. I ended up going back to Texas and started teaching and coaching in my old school district. It was a great choice for me. I loved this opportunity to impact the youth in a positive way. I saw my students graduate, get scholarships, compete at state meets, compete in college, and be great citizens and parents. I have been a teacher, coach, and assistant principal, and now I am going into my fifth year as a principal. I love what I do, and every day is different but impactful. I have the privilege of supporting students, teachers, support staff, etc. Reading this portion of my chapter, you will notice that I only mentioned the good things, the things that had a positive impact or impression on my life. Please do not misunderstand me. My life was not and is not even close to running this smooth and being this simple. I choose to focus my energy on what is positive and love all the great experiences and opportunities that have crossed my path.

I Love Me, So I Am Ready to Love You.

I have reached the point in my life where I have accomplished many things, and life has continued to move at a rate that is hard to keep up with at times. It is time for me to enjoy life with someone who will push and support me, challenge and question me, collaborate, and enjoy the time we have together. Someone that I can call my wife. Not too many people get a second chance at something as beautiful as love or as precious as a life partner. My wife and I have been friends for years. We started attending school together in the seventh grade. It wasn't until our senior year in high school that we really got to know each other. We had a few classes together, and we realized quickly that both of us knew we were going to college. We were on the same page about our education and knew it was necessary. We enjoyed our senior festivities like homecoming, prom, operation prom, senior picnic, class trips, etc. She would help me study for physics and any other class where I needed support. Maybe I was just trying to spend time with her; I will never tell. We would also spend time together hanging out and watching movies on the weekends. She was good for me, but we both had plans that would send us in different directions after graduation. She was going to Prairie View A&M University, and I was going to the University of Louisiana Lafayette. It was not the time to be selfish. I cared about her too much to go through a young long-distance relationship. As young adults, we needed to focus on school and our bright futures. We remained friends throughout our years in college, occasionally talking and seeing each other when I was in Houston visiting. Our friendship was forever-lasting, and we valued that relationship deeply.

We eventually went on with our lives, and the conversations went silent. She would soon be married, and so would I; our time had run out, and our lives had moved on. Years had passed, and my marriage was coming to an end. There was a mutual agreement between my wife and me that we would be better as friends. She needed to figure out some things, and she could not do that with me, so we agreed that our journey together was over. No hard feelings; we would remain, friends, because I choose to love. Years had passed, and little did I know my present wife was also going through a life-changing situation. She had finalized her divorce. Not knowing, I ended up moving close to the area where she lived, and we reconnected. We became workout partners, talked on the phone, and occasionally met up for lunch. It was amazing how we didn't miss a beat, and we had so many things in common. We still did not make any serious relationship moves, and she would say that was my fault. I don't think it was me, but I could be wrong. We both ended up in different relationships that did not work out, so now it was really on me. Enough was enough. I finally took the plunge to solidify us as a couple. She became my girlfriend, soon became my fiancé, and finally my wife. My love for this woman is unwavering and unconditional. Without a shadow of a doubt, she is the one for me because I continue to choose love.

Love is your choice. I stated this throughout this chapter. When you open your heart and allow yourself to love or be loved, you are opening up yourself to a chance at a great life filled with happiness.

Remember, love is not just the feelings you have for a significant other or a single individual. Love is about living your life with a caring, kind heart and choosing to be that positive energy that brings people together. Share that positive energy with the ones you interact with on a daily basis. Love is caring for those who cannot care for themselves and having critical conversations with those who need redirection or guidance. Love isn't always easy. You will go through your trials and tribulations, but love is worth it.

ABOUT THE AUTHOR:

Social Media:

IG @charleswoodsww

FB @charleswoodsww

Email ullgrad1911@hotmail.com

Charles Woods is a public-school building principal who leads with a positive mindset and a drive to support educators. He effectively supports young scholars in increasing their academic outcomes and developing strong social-emotional behaviors. Charles has eighteen years in public education, nine years as a classroom teacher and football coach, six years as a head boys track coach, five years as an assistant principal, and four years as a building principal.

Charles has an M.S. in Engineering and Technology Management and a B.S. in Industrial Technology from the University of Louisiana at Lafayette, where he received a full athletic scholarship and a graduate assistant scholarship. Charles was the football team captain during his senior year at the University of Louisiana at Lafayette. After his senior year, he returned to the university to be a graduate assistant football coach.

Charles Woods is a Best-Selling Author for his work with sixteen other gentlemen in The Impact of Influence, volume 1, Mentor, Coach, and Speaker.

His certifications include:

- EC - 12 Principal Certification
- EC -12 Special Education Certification

- Course work completed for Superintendent Certification.
- Rice University Leadership Partner's Executive Education Academy

Charles says there is no other profession that allows him the opportunity to impact lives like public education. He did not choose this path; this path chose him. He will continue to be a servant leader to those in his care and to those that choose to work with him. Charles is grateful for this opportunity to make a difference and mold our young scholars. Don't be a product of your environment; make your environment be a product of the positive you!

Quotes by: Charles Wood
1. "Don't assume anything and be prepared for everything!"
2. "Think GREAT!, Do GREAT!, Be GREAT!"
3. "Do Better, Be Better!"
4. "The grass is never greener; some grass needs more water."
5. "I live to serve; I don't serve to live."

TACOS, WINGS, AND SUBS

Jordan W. Adams

Hi, my name is Jordan Adams, and I am fourteen years old. I attend middle school in Baltimore County, Maryland. I have an advanced green belt in karate, and I love basketball. My favorite team is the Memphis Grizzlies. Ja Morant, number twelve, is one of my top three players on the team because he gets crazy dunks and contacts and got one chase-down block on the Lakers. You can find it on TikTok. It's worth the watch!

When I think about love, some of the first things that come to my mind are my favorite foods, noodles, burgers, and pizza. However, I could talk about basketball all day. I also wanted to discuss where I first learned about love. I love God because He loved me first and put me in a stable family with people that love and support me. My family loves me in bad times, good times, and scary times. They always have my back, and I thank God for them.

Another reason why I love God is because of all the sacrifices He made for us and how he died on the cross for our sins. God loves us and makes us new people when we follow him. That was the reason why I decided to get baptized. I wanted to change myself and start a new chapter in my life. God allows us all to do that at any time and any age. He always has our back.

I Love Basketball

What I love about basketball is how much fun it is and how much talent you need. I love it because it's cool and I am good at it. I have hops, I can play good defense, and I can shoot a little bit too.

My father introduced me to basketball when I was younger. It began when we played the game NBA 2K13 together, and we always had a good time. It is a basketball video game that you can buy on PS4, XBOX, PS5, and XBOX Series X. You can play it anytime, with anyone. I enjoy playing with my cousins, friends, teammates, and anyone who wants to play.

It has its ups and downs, but I'll give it a seven out of ten Overall, the games can be hard to play, but it's still fun.

When playing 2K, I usually play center because I love to get contacts and play great defense. I play other positions like shooting guard, small forward, and sometimes power forward. It never gets old, and I always have a good time. The PS4 version sucks, but the Next-Gen version on PS5 is great. The PS5 version has a whole city and all types of events. You can win items and buy stuff like clothes, shoes, and more. These are huge reasons why I love the game.

I Love My Family

It is easy to love when you have a good family. The things I love about my family are simple; they are lovely, funny people. First, I have my uncle Russell. He's my mom's brother. It's always fun when he comes back home to visit Maryland because he lives far away in Pennsylvania. Then there's my grandma; she has been there for me since I was born. When I was younger, I would go into her room and ask for icy pops. She always had the best flavors and would ensure I had one or two before I slept. Another family member that I loved was my grandfather. He was the best! I remember when my mom and I went to see him at work. We took many great pictures that day. It's one of my favorite memories of him. It's simple when I think about my dad and my mom; they have been there for me and always been by my side, and I thank them for that.

Love is in everyone. It can be serious, stupid, or whatever you want. You can scroll through TikTok or Netflix and see one thing that catches your eye and fall in love with a new page or a new show. You can tell how much you love a show when you binge-watch it nonstop. That shows the connection you can have, like love at first sight.

When I fall in love with my girlfriend, I want it to be a good experience. I want her to be able to cook, be cool, and have a goofy and cringy side. I hope that we will both love each other and match each other's energy. So many things in the world are difficult, bad, and mean, but you will feel better when you find that one thing that brings you joy. For me, playing games and basketball brings me joy.

If you do not have something that you love or that makes you happy, you can start something new like watching shows, listening to music, or even reading a book. There are many ways to be happy and positive because love is all around us; you just have to find it.

ABOUT THE AUTHOR:

Social Media:

IG @unboxingchange

Email hello@unboxingchange.com

Jordan Adams Frisby is a fourteen-year-old middle school student in Baltimore County, Maryland. Born on Christmas Day, he is currently an advanced green belt in karate and loves God, basketball, and food. Jordan's favorite team is the Memphis Grizzlies, and he enjoys tacos, wings, pizza, and more.

Jordan can talk about basketball all day, and he's not too bad as a player. He has hops, plays good defense, and can shoot a little bit. That's why he loves the game so much.

Jordan believes that there are many hard things in the world, but you will feel better when you find that one joy.

LOVE ENDURES THROUGH GROWTH

Ryan H. Dunston

I am Ryan Dunston. Before I mention my accomplishments, accolades, or professional titles, I would like to identify that I am a man of God, husband, father, son, brother, and uncle. I come out of a broken, single-mother household. I take time to note the hats I wear as a man of faith and family because it is the foundation and reason for the "why" I must grow. Growing is hard and painful. It can even be traumatizing, but it is overwhelmingly necessary. As adults, most of us can honestly say, growing is unavoidable. Time never stops, which means I must evolve and grow for my wife, children, and sphere of influence in every season of my life.

Growth looks different for everyone. I think there is value in pointing out the hidden details of change; I can also describe some of my experiences that prompted growth in my life, at the very least. Many times in my life, I needed to love God, myself, and my family enough to grow.

However, Love keeps you in the fight. I found my cycles of growth consisted of four significant components. The first three components are a failure, change, and anger. These three components are not experienced in any order, but wrestling with them leads to the last one, an agreement with God.

Anger

Let's start with one of the most challenging, lengthy, and ongoing fights in my life … anger. Anger was highly tricky for me. My battle with anger was not evident in the beginning. Things did not change until I began to ask myself some critical questions. What do you do when anger shows itself? Do you assess it? Depending on what you're angry over, do you place origin over it? I have learned that sourcing anger provides clarity and allows me to process my way to forgiveness. For me, anger has played a continuous role in my life, mainly because I have failed to source its foundation in my core. I have found my surface reaction to the sentiment intriguing as I reflect on anger. I can see that anger controls me, dictating my intense moments and injecting itself into my future. All because I have failed to assess it. Well … I have decided to take an in-depth look.

Lately, I have recognized my spirit wrestling my feelings into submission when anger shows itself. The submission of my feelings prepares my flesh for sacrifice for the sake of responsibly and sensibly stewarding over that current moment. I have begun to realize that when I can gain command over my feelings at that moment, I simultaneously gain command of my future. The fact that current moments impact our immediate and distant futures alludes to us when the emotion of anger arises and causes us to let go of the moments we are supposed to have dominion over. But why? That thought asks again, do you assess anger when it shows itself?

Anger is associated with numerous terms that will force you to open Pandora's Box when scrutinized correctly. The first term that stuck out to me was "antagonism." Anger is an emotion characterized by antagonism toward someone or something you feel has deliberately done you wrong. Thinking about this definition from an external standpoint seems natural. When someone or something has done you wrong, it is natural and healthy to express the negative emotion to avoid suppressing it, causing depression. But what about when you are angry at yourself? Do you associate it with where and who you came from?

The next term that piqued my interest as I explored anger is "antipathy." Antipathy is defined as a deep-seated feeling of dislike. In other words, resentment. Personally, when I analyzed negative emotions towards myself, I found the habits, hurt, tormented me, and trauma from which I came. This formed resentment and bitterness towards family members, childhood friends, and different races; this was sourced from being mistreated. My heart was hardened. As I made my way through life, the following happened:

- I buried the hurt which did not die. Instead, the damage grew roots and showed itself in my blind spots. I coped with it by unknowingly feeding the pain. I nourished my pain with substances and flirting, which made me feel better about myself while taking me away from reality.

- I avoided anything that forced me to confront my habits—even shrinking myself to the point that I would shelve my gifts to blend into the backward culture. Shrinking my gift also produced stagnation because it is the one thing that would bring me into challenging positions that would evolve me.

- I would not forgive the ones who caused the trauma. It added an enormous amount of weight and kept my perspective narrow; this created a small, minded understanding.

Going through life, I realized I learned how to live with my pain. But learning how to live with the resentment formed unknown triggers that would ignite me in moments when certain things reminded me of the habits I could not break, the hurt I could not un-feel, and the trauma I thought I buried. That brings me to the following term, "contention."

Contention is defined as heated disagreements. But how do they happen? I found in nearly every argument I have had sourced to a rooted issue, sourced forgotten trauma, or someone forcing me to confront a negative habit I was not prepared to break. And not because I did not want to but because either I did not see it (blind spot) or I did not know how to break it, which was even more frustrating. It was not until I noticed and analyzed everything that things began to get better.

There is no secret potion or medicine to take to heal. In my opinion, the treatment for anger is, to be honest with yourself and acknowledge it. Acknowledging it allows you to become aware of the situation. It will also allow you to change your response organically. When you have analyzed and combed through the origin of the anger, you will learn your triggers. You also take the breaks needed when your anger is triggered, and you will forgive when necessary.

Failure

Failure was a component I misunderstood for a long time. But once I got my arms around failure, my perspective of it changed dramatically. The Google English Dictionary[1] defines failure in two different ways. The first defines failure "as a lack of success." Although this definition can be evident to some, I encourage you to take a second look. I used to accept that definition as absolute, and as a result, the risk I took was limited. I found safety in choosing less risk, which developed unforeseen complacency and a lack of growth. I was once told that still water produces infection while flowing water washes it away. Honestly, I believe this to be true via personal experience. I also think failure speaks to you, which brings me to the second definition.

---

[1] Google search. Google. Accessed May 2022. https://www.google.com/search?client=firefox-b-1-d&q=failure.

The Google English Dictionary also defines failure as the omission of expected or required action. Some synonyms that go along with this definition are negligence, neglect, and oversight. Failure provides direction to you in its rejection of whatever circumstance you are experiencing it in. Applying accountability to this definition, you ask yourself crucial questions like what did I miss (oversight)? Did I let go of how I thought it should be done (unintentional negligence and neglect)? Within contemplation, you begin to grow. The term "failure" begins to minister to you rather than feeling like a death sentence. If you submit to the obedience failure is asking you to incorporate, you can use it as a compass to success. Changing the way I perceive failure interpretation of my efforts has most certainly accelerated my growth; and has also relieved me of my self-sabotaging thoughts. If your thoughts are negative, your feelings will also be negative. If your emotions are negative, it can be hard to start again. Allow failure to shape your success and have a say in your process. If you do, your evolution will pleasantly surprise you.

Change

Change is the last of the first three components. Honestly, I am not sure we thoroughly understand change. Cognitively, we use the word with a definition in mind; but I feel some of us may underestimate what it takes to change ourselves. Nevertheless, I believe change is needed. It pushes us to commit to the next level. As we reserve to the next level, change surfaces gifts deep within us to produce profound innovativeness (power) that we did not know we had. To put it plainly, you find out who you are in change.

Change can also be traumatic. I have been forced to change multiple times and in various ways over the last three years. There will be painful moments, but those moments are needed to strengthen yourself and be required for a purpose. I found some things about myself in my change that I did not know I had. Gifts I did not think I possessed. Stretched ... is the best way I can put it; stretched to develop resilience and to increase capacity to hold more responsibility. I stretched to learn that we have the power to turn a challenging situation to our advantage.

Do you experience failure in change? Most definitely! Failure is a part of the process. Change uses failure to shape you. Although change will force you to manage your emotions, fail forward, and stretch, it can be intimidating; you begin to find yourself living more once you press through it all. You get to experience more, learn more, have more fun, and pour into more people.

You must allow change. Allowing is hard! You must step out of your comfort zone to enable change to form your future. I laugh when I reflect on the growth, the impact, and witness (soak in) the new rooms I've been placed in, all because of change.

An Agreement with God

As a man, loving God, myself, and my family enough to manage my anger, allow failure to adjust my approach, and embrace change, has brought me into an agreement with God, which is my last component. I want to leave you with a prayer of understanding. A prayer of submission and empathy. My contract with Father God on how to humbly love me, my family, and the rest of his children.

Father, great God that you are, I thank you for the things that I do not understand. I kneel before you to confess my brokenness. Please forgive my flesh, emotions, feelings, and unwillingness to let go of the way to purpose. I am plagued with the remembrance of knowing when it feels like I am failing you, your people, and my family. The memory of knowing what it is to feel like your Kingdom and my family are better without me. The recollection of pondering over the thoughts of taking my own life due to how I see myself. I thought I had moved past these feelings and thoughts. I can see now that this latest shift in my life is surfacing buried pain. I am in awe, analyzing and confessing the depth of buried pain rooted in my heart. Father, how do I calm the rage flowing through me due to the mental torture I thought I was passed. How do I deal with the fears made present in my life at this moment? The fear of falling backward. The fear of losing ground. The fear of mishandling the giving cross, burden, and responsibility given to me. The fear of relinquishing control over my life. The fear of truly following in the dark. The fear of confronting the portions of myself I have unknowingly ignored for so long. Although painful, my yes has placed me in your hands for crafting. For surgery, for healing yet again.

Father, how do I discern against the enemies' illusions as you redirect my path. The enemy is taking opportunities to attack as you lead me down unforeseen paths. Breathe on my understanding so that I may fight back with what I know to be true about you, Father. Remind me daily of your presence in the change of plans so that I may rest in your redirection. Please provide comfort in my discomfort. Please calm my rage due to the sudden turn and change in direction you have decided to take me.

Father, as you reveal portions of me that are hurt in this season, please sit on my heart as I come to grips with the revelation that there is no progress without going through; there is no overcoming without obstacles and resistance, and there is no healing without inconvenience.

As I press forward, I notice that you are providing me with the revelation of more profound empathy and understanding for He was raised by a single mother which helped him develop strong moral grounds for love, loyalty, and respect. He is a father of five amazing children, Savanah, Joshua, Symone, Shamiya, and Avah. Every day Adrian is looking to make himself smarter, stronger, and better than he was yesterday. He wrote this in hopes of helping others realize that sometimes love doesn't fit into society's perfect story or definition. It can be a hard rocky road. Love, like most of us, is not all perfect for *your children— empathy is needed for the assignment we spoke about previously. I am noticing you're providing the purpose of the shift. I'm starting to understand further what you meant when you stated, "the pain you will feel when you awaken is not about you. Do not forget to remember ... Remember me when you feel it. Remember who I am to you when you feel this pain you have no understanding of." Thinking now with clarity, although extremely uncomfortable, I get it. I can now apply understanding to this season. I understand now that you are not punishing me but equipping me with more power, downloading more wisdom into me for the mission in your kingdom. I must confess with an unselfish heart I have a new understanding of the phrase, "when you understand, you can't say but." You have told me before that "why's matter" and that my "why will be stronger than my willpower."*

Father, provide me with the patience to wait as you continue to reveal to me the depths of my heart. Provide the patience to wait as you continue to add more capacity to my heart. Provide me with the strength to endure as you show me how to love your children as they go through their transitions.

Provide me the strength to endure as your children may reject your way, as I have, at first but follow eventually with revelation. Provide me with the hope and endurance needed for me to persevere and to love your children through their healing process.

Father, I am, as always, available for glory. And even now, through tears, I write to you ... Praying through the written word ... expressing the pain but also the truth of sacrifice. Love endures, and I love you, my family, and your children through it all. My sacrifice of the flesh is now before you. I am now able

to say to you; I thank you for what I now understand. In Jesus'
name ... For your kingdom ... Have your way ... Amen.

Love endured over time as I became Ryan Dunston:

- Community Outreach Coordinator and Brand Ambassador for HomeTown Lenders
- Host of "The Ryan Dunston Podcast ... Words from a Humble King" Founder of True Kings non-profit
- Mentor
- A man of God
- Loving husband to my wife, Patrice Dunston
- Father to my sons, Jahlil, Ryan, and Cameron
- Son to my mother, Piper Dunston
- And now an author

Life is still going....

ABOUT THE AUTHOR:

Social Media:

IG @ryan_dunston_

FB @ryan.dunston.7

Email ryan.dunston@htlenders.com

Ryan Dunston is a Community Outreach Coordinator & Brand Ambassador for HomeTown Lenders. He is the Founder of the Non-profit True Kings and The Ryan Dunston Podcast *Words from a Humble King*. Ryan sits on the board of the Non-profit Y-Knot Inc. and is the Co-owner of Dunston & Associations LLC.

Ryan is tremendously knowledgeable about all residential mortgages and finance and has an extensive customer/community service background. He has a unique and undeniable passion for people. Born to a single mother and raised in East Baltimore, Maryland, Ryan is a devoted husband and father of three boys, ultimately reflecting his humble family-oriented mindset that fuels his approach to serving any present needs. Ryan believes that love heals … and Love is how he serves.

TRANSITIONING LOVE

Nailah "Sunnie" Jones

Love is a four-letter word with many meanings. What love is for me may not be love for you. I learned this during one of the most significant transitional journeys in my life.

As a young black transman, you are tested during your journey, and love, showing, creating, giving, and receiving are among them. If I had talked about love in the past, you would probably think it was nonexistent for me. I wanted to love others the way I wanted to be loved. It wasn't at the forefront of my worries regarding relationships. However, that all changed when I met Jazmyne. Being trans on its own and finding love is hard, but being black and trans is different. I have been blessed to find someone who acknowledges and sees me as me. Jazmyne loves me as me!

Jazmyne and I were high school sweethearts, good friends who became lovers. But I've always known that I loved Jaz. So, something felt different when we rekindled during the summer of 2020. When we started to relearn each other, I quickly learned that

I had to change my perspective on love. I knew if I wanted this relationship to be fruitful, I had to change how I give love. I could not love her the way I wanted to be loved but had to love her the way she needed or wanted to be loved.

Being on testosterone for over a year and transitioning into my pure form has not been easy. I am going through puberty again. I've relearned so much and how to cope and adjust to the new me. I think of love now as happiness, laughter, forgiveness, and fun. Sometimes, we look at love as something that seems unreachable, but I learned that everyone's situation is different. Love for me may not be love for you. Being on something that affects my mind more than my physical appearance took a toll. I fought one side of my brain with the other, and I saw new lights as I continued to fight.

I know relationships have obstacles, and with what we have gone through in two years, only love could have bought us through it. I would never change anything that I have encountered in my relationship. Through every obstacle, I can sit back and see the positivity in the situation. I can see and feel the love. It took communication and understanding; we had to compromise and be honest. Jazmyne and I overcame obstacles as little as what we were going to eat to things as big as if we would take the next steps in our relationship. In the moments of confusion, sadness, anger, and uncertainty, I learned that Black love is real.

As I grasped this concept, understanding love languages played a significant role. Knowing each one is important. Words of affirmation, gift-giving/receiving, acts of service, physical touch, and quality time. Learn these six things and then learn which one is your partner and how they want to be loved. It will change you entirely. It will bring you closer, and it will bring back the spark. When I sat and learned myself and then my partner, our dying spark reignited and hasn't burnt out.

Love is a four-letter word that is forever changing—a four-letter word with many meanings and reasons. I'm still grasping the concept of love as a twenty-year-old man. I know I will continue to learn love as I further my transition as a Black man. My mindset of love has changed as anything would when you have a drastic change towards love.

ABOUT THE AUTHOR:

Social Media:

IG @sunniedeelite

Email info@middlemanfirm.com

Nailah "Sunnie" Jones is a Goucher College Alumni from Prince George's County, Maryland. He currently resides in Columbia, Maryland. Sunnie earned a Bachelor of Arts in Computer Science but has always had a passion for entrepreneurship and arts. He now works as a software engineer and as a programs manager. He had begun his career in film, where he has recently produced a documentary and is currently working on his docu-series. Additionally, Sunnie will soon be published as an author for the upcoming book "Black Men Love" which will be released in May 2022. Along with Sunnie's professional gains, he has been going through a big transition. During these last two years, Sunnie has found his true identity as a transman. This discovery of himself has pushed Sunnie, his mom, and a close family friend to start a non-profit for parents and families of those in the trans community. Sunnie hopes to touch many in his life with light and wisdom!

YELLOW LOVE

Daniel McMaster

I love you. You might not know it because you have moved on, but I love you. You taught me that I didn't love myself and that it was required to love myself before I could love for real.

I love her. She was an electric shock to my system that rests through the portals of my eyes. It was the first time I saw you. I was in love. I love you. The ideas you brought forward in me became the foundation of my life.

I love him. For the time I knew you, you opened me up to a world that I had not known before. You showed me the flaws that others found as virtues.

I loved him. Despite my betrayal over and over throughout the years, you were the one who defended me against my insecurities and allowed me to pretend I was as good as you for far too long. Or, as far back as I remember, there was nothing that could separate us.

I love you. Your strength made me brave enough to face my fears. I have not found the words to tell you0 I forgive you, but I love you. The one that got away the specter of my dreams, I see you and walk with you and hold your hand in times of sadness and sorrow. I love you. For all the times she touched me in ways that I couldn't see myself as worthy. I love you. The time we shared in the cramped apartment fighting mice and mold.

I love you. The man who taught me that a man is an end unto himself and that the scales of justice are weighed against the work I produce and that I am free of the expectations of others. I love you because I love myself. The less that I wished as of this writing but more than I ever have, free from the burden of those who are "better" than me in my mind...I am in love, blanketed by the cacoon of its safety and comforted by its warmth. I love.

Yellow love

Yellow is my favorite color. In the third grade, I decided that yellow was my favorite color. It is a beautiful color, bright and vibrantly full of energy. But I was also eight, and somehow, I concluded that yellow was a gay color. Coming from a mildly conservative Christian Jamaican household, being gay was unacceptable. So, I ultimately didn't accept it. I rejected the idea completely and with totality, so far as to even change my favorite color to orange. I loved orange. It is the energy of yellow mixed with the masculinity of red. The fire of rage and strength. Red was too much, but orange was the compromise I was looking for in the end.

Orange was a color that I could get behind. Adapting to social forces has become a sort of superpower of mine. Creating connections between seemingly innocent objects and perverse anecdotes was what I prided myself in. Say a word, and I can make it sexual. A pencil looks like a penis. The bicycle has two wheels that look like breasts with little nipples at the anchor. I was in elementary school. I cleaned up. Innocent enough at the time, quite cringy now. But that was before I found porn—1996 was a simpler time. The internet was young but not devoid of its dark corners. Porn was an entryway into a world I didn't know existed. There was so much to explore, and it awakened something very primal in me. Interestingly enough, it was the imagining over the different scenes because of the time's tech limits. The internet was slow, and even though there was porn available in the form of video, feature-length porn was an overnight ordeal. Set it and forget it. Pick a movie, hit download, and come back looking for what you got the next day. The best I could get for instant gratification was trailers. With a trailer, you could download in twenty agonizing minutes with an erection, but it was better than enduring the agony of downloading trash. Porn was a secret soundtrack to middle school. A productive time for me academically, I could find time to sneak to the family computer to jerk off at my convenience. For a time, this was enough until the flame of my desire waned for busty blondes and Asian beavers. I wanted something more fulfilling, something that took me on a journey. That is when I found erotica. Cheerleaders who convinced a jock to come behind the bleachers, and they would take turns sucking his dick, only to fight over who would go last to get cum on. It was a classic coming-of-age story. But this merely lays the groundwork for my story.

Fast forward through busty teenagers and morning erections, I tucked into the belt of my pants and checked out the ass and panties of the girl who sat in front of me for the better part of four years in high school until age seventeen. By now, I had spent countless hours scouring the internet, preparing for the moment when I would lose my virginity. Growing up in a moderately conservative, Christian Jamaican household and addicted to porn, my virginity was a crossroads. I hadn't decided if I would give it away or hold onto it for marriage. This nondecision came to a head when I was lying on a couch next to a beautiful, busty babe two years my senior from an entirely different country. Less than deciding, this opportunity took me along for the ride. In the darkness of the living room, I slid my erection home to glory. But the victory was short-lived. Putting away the joy of what I had just accomplished was replaced by soul-crushing guilt and shame. I immediately called long distance to speak with my friend in the Christian Youth Group and cry over the sin I had just committed. I was distraught. And that was the birth of my sex. But not my love. Love was tricky for me. Unfortunately, I was never honest with my friends about my sexuality. They were teenagers, and it was simple enough to lie about the things I did and who I did them with. Pride was a huge factor in my decision-making. And although they were fine people, I could not leverage their advice because I was not honest with them. Exaggerating my exploits and prowess left no room for a real conversation about what life is. My religious household was less than helpful in being my authentic self because my parents had insane discipline and self-assurance to create an environment where perfection was possible, and that was the standard that I was to live up to as a young adult. The technical term was" backsliding." I would also later learn that it was called being a carnal Christian, someone who was Christian but behaved and acted as "the world" does. Sleeping around and "shaking up" the roads manifested by the trauma of losing my virginity was never resolved. When I got home, swearing I would never do it again and would wait until marriage, I quickly found myself slapping genitals with a neighborhood girl, and the flood gates were opened slightly. You see, missing out and even going far as judging those who were trying to figure out their own high school lives did not form the proper brain channels to figure out how to create a sexual situation for me. Instead, I manipulate my way into the hearts and subsequently the pants of several women. I can recall stories upon stories.

One Year as a Woman

This is the story of my coming of age. It all started in elementary school when I was deciding on my favorite color. I liked yellow and thought it was my favorite. The very next thought was that yellow is a gay favorite color. I changed my favorite color to orange. Orange had the energy of yellow with a splash he rages, a definitively masculine trait. This is the first time I lied to society to be accepted, but it wouldn't be the last.

For my next trick, I will make anything you say, perverted. I was connecting the dots between a pencil and a penis. Between a cup and your mother's butt. I was a hit in my Northeastern Baltimore elementary school. All the kids thought I was so clever. Turning tricks for their entertainment, I wasn't doing any of the stuff; I was a fraud. But they couldn't know it. I was riding the high of the attention. Need me, you bevy of incompetent inferiors. Worship me with your cheers and laughter. This was not my thought process at ten; I was more of a big grin and slow and sure dissociation between what I knew I was taught I needed to be to play the game. I learned early on that I could get another hit of dopamine by being successful at school, fortunately.

I learned early on that I could get another hit of dopamine by being successful at school, fortunately. I had two parents who could facilitate that by being smart themselves. They had a Ph.D. and a Master's between them, so my questions were answered in a calm and receptive way. It allowed for the principles to be obtained, both in the moment and years later when I was thinking about the subject in a different context. It allowed for an excellent environment for learning. I hated doing the work of learning because a lot of it came very quickly for me. And this caused me to take shortcuts. I would skim and cheat the information into my brain and do the processing during the test. The backside of this theory is that it caused me tremendous amounts of anxiety. I would be deathly afraid of the test-taking process. That was the start of my crippling anxiety (to be discussed later.)

You see, on paper, I had the ideal home: two loving and committed parents, annual vacations, plenty of food, and shelter. I lived in a mildly conservative Christian Jamaican religious household. It was great. It came with all the trimmings, church on Sunday, prayer every night, setting out your clothes Saturday evening to prepare for the next, and mildly persistent homophobia. It was the nineties, and in truth, the world was different; masculinity was such that the threat of being accused of being gay was this stigma that required an individual to fight for the respect taken from him. It was a pseudonym for poor performance and general ineptitude. But that didn't bother me. I laughed and joked right along with the rest; I wasn't gay, and being bisexual is the same as being gay. But sometimes, I would defend homosexuals referenced in the conversation. "Does wanting to wear a dress make you gay? It is a piece of clothing. Successfully covering your nakedness. That being said, looking terrible in a dress is unacceptable."

The problem with lies is that they create a fork between who you are and how you appear. Coming from a mildly conservative Jamaican Christian household, the party line is quite clear. Do good in school, go to college, get married, and have babies. The tricky thing about this is when you have an idea of your own—one that is not in line with the party's position—you have to make a choice. You can fight the power, or you can get in line. The issue comes when you are fighting an opponent on their turf. In high school, I was interested in working in the lab in downtown Baltimore. It was an opportunity to do natural science that applied something that I could build a life on in the real world. I wanted to go. I asked and was refused. I made my case that I would learn so much and that it would not be an issue for me to leave school early and take the light rail downtown and work for a few hours. The answer was no. At that point, my will to fight against the will of others was significantly diminished. That, combined with the lies that made up my personality, were significant factors that led me to serve my female GF for a year, taking a traditional woman's role.

So, in the beginning, I thought I was going to have a baby, turns out it wasn't mine; I have had three pregnancy scares in my lifetime, and this one was not going to be like the other ones; I was going to be there for the baby and the mother. I got played for months on end. This chick strung me along and told me that her baby was mine. It is the conflict between the chance that it is mine and the abandoning someone in their time of need. It's none of my business. I have always had a bleeding heart for the disenfranchised. There is an issue that causes more issues later on in life. I found someone who matched my sexuality and traded her for someone I felt could give me the life I wanted. I was turned on by what I thought was my perfect match.

One Year Later...

Confusion begets confusion, and we are at war, but I am losing. I have no moral grounds to justify my outrage regarding child-rearing to sex. I do not command respect in my own home, and things come to a head when I have no recourse except violence. The question that is often asked in the case of violence is whether the individual should have just left. There is no way to balance the equation when you feel powerless to affect change with someone who says they are giving their all to make you happy. The math doesn't add up. By this time, the conflict surrounding her ex has come to a head.

I came out to my parents, hurt, ashamed, confused, ejected, and rejected. I felt pressured to prove a point but accepted the idea altogether. The nature of bisexuality is an open to sexual experience without the restriction of gender; this is, to me, a function of loving your neighbor.

ABOUT THE AUTHOR:

Social Media:

IG @being_mcmaster

FB @Sedulous.Gentleman

Email danielpmcmaster@gmail.com

Daniel McMaster was born in Baltimore, Maryland, to two Jamaican emigrants; he led a life of adventure and education. He graduated with honors from the Prestigious Baltimore Polytechnic Institute. Daniel received an undergraduate degree from the University of Maryland Baltimore County and a Master's in Systems Engineering from George Washington University. He does not like to define the nature of his passion projects as it limits who and what he is, although Daniel serves his community's needs as they evolve and grow.

CHEVY

Joseph Henry

We've all heard someone say that life is the ultimate teacher; however, love is a professor if life is a teacher. Love provides depth, context, and motivation that sustains life. Love provides passion where all else is lost. Love is the gentle wind that hits your face during autumn sunrises and late summer sunsets—moments of renewal, perspective, and purpose. There is no greater love than to lay down one's life—a higher power when it's done for the people. We've had countless soldiers lay down their lives for the progress of our community. Many we know, Malcolm, Martin, and Garvey, all laid it bare for us, but there are lesser-known and often forgotten that we owe so much more, the grocery clerk, the trash man, and the barber.

I remember the day I fell in love for the first time. I can recall it like an old episode of 227. The sights, sounds, and smells; you can just take it all in. The freedom to just be—to be seen and heard on my own. I was not knowing until that day that it was even a desire— my beloved. The safety of being amongst and around the people is a feeling we should all experience, not just thinking but knowing you belong.

These feelings are often fleeting, the connection that comes with seeing people like you, living a total departure from the narratives found on the TV screen. Sitcoms and music videos often portray my beloved as less than and never relatively equal, but always separate. Unity was an idea that could be achieved in theory but was never quite real.

That wasn't the case in the chocolate city. Doctors, lawyers, dentists, and teachers are plenty in the same neighborhood as the grocery clerk and the trashman. Shade tree mechanics, librarians, and pushers all existed, even commingled together.

Every city has a vibe; it's the flare that makes it unique and unlike any other. In a chocolate city, that was excellence. Black Excellence! Strength and resilience that came from a class of people known as civil servants were often shaped by civil disobedience. Goodness was not to strive for ultimately; it was expected. That's what made DC so beautiful, a city filled to the brim with Black people who loved, honored, and at any moment, we were ready to give it all for their people.

Walking out of my grandmother's house was common but usually accompanied by a one-block limit. Just far enough for me to have a sense of independence but close enough that I could hear my grandmother call from the back porch; where she spent time in the summer, speed-coursing word searches and crossword puzzles while she watched her stories and old reruns of *Are You Being Served*—the British sitcom based upon the haphazard management of a department store. But one particular day, it was a little different. I would get my first taste of freedom.

Unbeknown to me, it was a test. One that I would both fail and pass with flying colors. I could admit this freely now as my beloved grandmother has gone home to be with the Lord, although I am still fully convinced that Jesus may make an exception if she asked to hit me one more time with her cane. Anyway, back to it. That was the day I would walk to the barbershop on my own.

We all know the barbershop's place in the hearts of any Black community. These are pillars in every Black community, places where we gather without fear, fraternize, receive counsel, and often exist. If you listen and pay attention, the barbershop will give you an unrivaled education by any ivy institution—business, finance, psychology, and eschatology in one conversation. Try finding that in any course offered at Princeton.

As I set out on my journey, I had no idea that a simple ten-block walk would be a formative experience. It is essential to highlight that my feeling of freedom was utterly inaccurate, as I would later learn there were spies on my route. But that's a discussion for another time; my grandmother's neighborhood network was not a game, and I'm not convinced an MI6 could do better.

Walking out of the house, I noticed the Delts, our neighbor's five houses down. Now, everyone knew the Delts because they were extremely nice, well-to-do professionals who never seemed too busy to say hi. I knew the Delts, however, because of my girlfriend, Zaria.

Technically, it didn't count because she was ten years older and a sophomore at Howard. We never officially dated, officially unofficially, but that didn't stop me from trying. Her dog, Napoleon, however, did. This behemoth of a canine was the size of a small mountain. And from time to time, he would get loose. But is any childhood complete without the fear of being eaten by your not-so-friendly neighborhood rottweiler? I swear that dog used to laugh.

"Hey, Zaria!" "Hey, little man!" "I'm going to get a haircut." Alright now. Heart racing! Now it was time to focus on not falling down the stairs. Success! I didn't even stumble. Now, I smoothly walk down the block. I remember wondering if my cousin was home upon getting to the corner. He lived on the next block. Maybe I'd check on the way back as I made my way down 3rd street.

"Hey, little man!" "Hey, Mr. Marshall." Mr. Marshall served with the red tails and boxed in the Army. He was outside wiping down his car or smoking a cigar on his front porch if he was breathing. Mr. Marshall knew everyone in the neighborhood, sometimes better than they knew themselves, and he was always watching. A protector was just who he was. He did it out of his love for the people.

"Hey, little man!" "Hey, Mr. Plum!" "What is that weird-looking rake?" "Ohhh, this is no ordinary rake. This, little man, is a seed planter?" Now, I should have known better than to ask Mr. Plum anything, and I certainly, knew better than to ask when I had somewhere to be. Mr. Plum was our neighborhood historian, filled with more useless facts than a ten-time Jeopardy champion. He may as well have been known as a Black Alex Trebek. "This seed planter was invented by a man named Henry. Just like you, little man. Did you know that?" Of course not how the hell was I supposed to know that. "No, sir, I did not." "Well, let me tell you a bit about it." I took a seat on the stoop of his brownstone; even Stevie Wonder could see this would be a while. Mr. Plum proceeded to tell me all about Henry Taylor and how he had roots in Maryland and was born a free man. Mr. Plum took pride in educating anyone willing to listen. He would always say to remember what he said at the end of every conversation because a man could only go as far as his education. He did it for the love of the people.

As I continued on my journey, I came across Mr. Odell. He went to the city as part of the great migration. Like many, he served in the military, and he was a sailor during the Korean war. Mr. Odell was a sharecropper before joining the Navy. Every summer, he would grow enough food to last all winter on a four hundred-square-foot plot. "Where you headed, boy?" "The barbershop." "Make sure you come on over here and get your grandmother some tomatoes on your way back." "Thank you, Mr. Odell." He would always send a little with you on your way. He was all about self-sufficiency and taking care of your neighbor. He did it because of his love for the people.

What is that beautiful noise? As I prepared to cross Missouri Avenue, I heard an unmistakable voice. He was affectionately known as the Godfather of Go-Go. Now Chuck Brown is a chocolate city icon with bobblehead figurines and DC lottery endorsements to prove it. But long before he was mainstream, he was simply known as Chuck. If you said Chuck, you could only be talking about Wind

Me Up. He embodied everything DC used to be, resilient people who knew how to party, even in the face of adversity. Community cookouts and Georgia Avenue days. Chuck was a staple that showed us all how to love. He did it for the love of the people.

Eventually, overtaken by the beat, I found myself way off course. The barbershop was within reach, but I couldn't walk away from the joyful noise. It filled my soul and moved my feet before I knew I was two blocks off course, rocking to the beat. Street pharmacists and morticians, both surrounded by death, found life in Go-Go. We all did. Go-Go has a way of piercing the soul. Built off funk magnificently paired with Afro-Caribbean beats, Go-Go was a genre all on its own and, for all the chocolate city's diaspora, the sweet sound of home.

I found myself in a foreign territory. My grandmother would murder me if she saw me, and rightfully so. The irony of the prospect of familial homicide in front of a funeral home is still well ironic. Suddenly, I found myself surrounded by smells, sounds, and feelings that overtook me. Aromas of pork ribs and cornbread escaped from the BBQ hut, rivaled by four pieces and mumbo sauce smells. Police sirens and firetrucks blared as they whizzed by. Pontiac Trans-Am's bellowed their exhaust, NOI brother selling papers and bean pies, evangelizing sudden death and determination to passersby. It was my city, and it flung my heart wide. These were my people. Ohh heavens, the time.

I looked down at my watch, and nearly two hours had gone by quickly. Surely my grandmother would be expecting me home in a short time. I hadn't even made it to the barbershop. Overcome with panic, I sprinted to the barbershop. Mrs. Williams exclaimed, "Boy, where have you been. Hurry up and get in this chair." Mrs. Williams was a bit of a trailblazer. A female barber in the eighties was not common. She had a quaint little two-chair shop filled with old ebony and jet magazines in the window where I'd sit and people watch. I looked forward to the beauty of the week and wondered how they always went to Howard. But today, for that, there would be no time. She didn't charge a lot of money; she always said, "Can you really put a price on dignity?" She was a lot more than a barber to many guys, and she was giving out a lot more than haircuts. She was a mother to some and auntie to others, but always an advocate keeping a watchful eye because of her love for the people.

"Now you get on back home before your grandmother worries." I bolted out the door with Chuck Brown playing in my head. "Run, Joe!" And run I did. Recounting all the events of what seemed like days but really was only about three hours.

That day I learned a lot about life. More importantly, I learned what love for people is all about. To truly love is to lay down one's life. Not in some grandiose fashion, but practically.

The Delts taught me that to love the people is to stay rooted in your community; to love the people is to remain amongst the people.

Mr. Marshall taught me to protect the ones I love by any means necessary and always keep a watchful eye. To watch over the people is to love the people.

Mr. Plum taught the importance of not just knowing yourself but where you come from and the importance of celebrating achievements. They don't need to be your achievements, and a step forward is a step in the right direction for us all. Mr. plum also taught that love requires patience. To love your people is to accept them where they are and motivate them to move forward by educating themselves, not by degrees and formalities but by partnering with one another.

Mr. Odell taught service, provision, and charity. Too often, we devote our talents outside of our communities when the real need lies within. Doing what we can for one another is enough. I can only imagine how many people he kept from going hungry on that twenty by twenty plot. To love the people is to feed the people, their bodies, their spirits, and their souls.

Chuck taught us all how to find joy in the pain. In the summer of 1989, Chocolate City earned a new name—Murder Capital; by 1991, we racked up a new record of 479; this was a painful time made by tumult, but Chuck carried us through it all. Music taught me to love the pain. We often run from it and hide from it, but we must embrace it to overcome it. The power to overcome lies within us all, and to love the people demands that we do.

The smells of BBQ taught us all the power of accepting what you're given and making it something special even when it is expected that one cannot. Tenderizing tough cuts of meat over low fire for extended periods is reflective of life. Go through the fire, and you'll have an experience with which you can nourish your people on the other side.

Mrs. Williams taught us to take pride in ourselves and walk with dignity. The power of a fresh cut. Many people walked into her shop downtrodden and walked out with superpowers. To love the people is to serve the people with what you have been given.

I fell in love with our beautiful Black people in the summer of 1991, and I've never looked back. To love the people is to give and to live. Give what you can give as you live. No matter the circumstance, no matter the odds, Black people will always rise. And for that, I love you—my beautiful Black people.

ABOUT THE AUTHOR:

Social Media:

IG @lionstrategic

Email jos.a.henry@gmail.com

JOSEPH HENRY, provides analytics, advice, and coaching to address blind spots and challenges within workplace cultures. He designs and executes custom interventions to achieve the desired organizational change for government and industry clients.

Joseph is fascinated by organizational culture and partners with his clients in the creation of inclusive, equitable workspaces. As a wellbeing consultant, Joseph helps organizations understand the value of a life well lived and how psychological safety drives performance and organizational evangelism.

Joseph has worked as a consultant in the areas of DE&I, Business Continuity (COOP) Emergency Management, Security and National Defense.

Joseph holds a master's degree in Organizational Leadership from Saint Mary's University of Minnesota, where he researched the impacts of Stereotype Threat and a bachelor's degree in Sociology & Anthropology from Towson University.

SELF LOVE

Sergio Vibetrill

Over time the concept of love as a Black man has revealed itself to be so many things to me. Love comes in all types of different experiences. Unfortunately, it's hard to get a grasp of it most of the time because you must be very cautious out there.

We live in a world where the word love is used so loosely. For some, the experience can be beautiful, and for others, the experience might be a nightmare. One thing is for sure for any sensible human being, love has to be genuine no matter who you are. What I noticed in my life is that the more you focus on self-love, the more genuine your love is when it comes to giving it out to those who are willing to accept it and not abuse it.

My personal experiences have led me to learn that love can bring a layer of complicated issues when there is a lack of communication with more than one party (that one party being you).

I believe that "self-love" is the best starting point for those who fall short of their insecurities.

I was fortunate enough to come from a lovely family of five. I've been able to recognize unconditional love since age four. As nature would have it, I was blessed with a loving mother to show me that type of love first. So, as I grew into a man, my biggest obstacle was trying not to give my love to the wrong people who would abuse the benefits of my most valuable possession I have to share.

By taking time to develop self-esteem, I've been able to discover new ways to connect with people and apply the right amount of love. Growing up, I realize that the key to human relations is to be more proactive when it comes to dealing with people who genuinely have a love for you. That philosophy allows me to manage my emotions well when things tend to look rocky amongst my peers. It gets complicated balancing out the types of love to maintain for people as human beings.

Coming up as a young man, my dad was the definition of hard love. My dad showed a militant type of love. It wasn't the most positive display, but he was there to do his part as a father. So that played a huge part in my discipline. While my mom was quite the opposite, she opened my eyes to the warm love of a mother. That form of love later recirculated into the same love that I show my kids as a father today.

My parents have always been the best example of love in the form of romance. I've seen what goes into thirty-five years of being married—the beautiful moments down to their most stressful moment dealing with each other. Growing up in a home such as mine, I felt inspired to duplicate the same family structure and love between my ideal wife and me that my parents showed to each other.

Needless to say, I've come to learn that we're currently living in is easier dreamed about than done, in my opinion. That's because it's damn near impossible to predict someone's true intentions accurately. So often, we're too busy being too skeptical of the "what ifs" scenarios that can plague our minds into thinking that finding someone capable of returning the same affection is impossible.

However, I like to be optimistic when thinking about my journey to discovering true love. I believe it's around the corner for me. All I must do is continue to show love and try to keep an open eye out for red flags that can signal when the love isn't beneficial for my mental health.

ABOUT THE AUTHOR:

Social Media:

IG @sergio.vibetrill

FB @sergio.cotti.50

Email t.wealthy13@gmail.com

Sergio Vibetrill is the owner of Luxurious Hustle, LLC. He is an independent father who is thriving as a digital entrepreneur and business enthusiast. Sergio started his journey as an entrepreneur in 2012. He managed to grow into a motivational influencer from those earlier years to now by studying personal development in health, wealth, love, and happiness.

MY VIEWPOINT

Robert Tyree

Seeing her grandparents inspired me to want to fall in love again. From my point of view, marriage is an unknown word, which is rarely seen, spoken of, or maintained. Marriage is considered malicious, unwanted, or untenable to the X Generation. I used to laugh at the thought of getting married because I never saw a successful partnership that could or desired to withstand the test of time. When I hear the word marriage, thoughts of singleness mixed with baby mommy drama, with a dash of bitterness and hate, ruin the potential or any further opportunities to desire the most amazing union desired by the flesh. Has the world glorified cheating, fighting, sex, and independence so much that marriage is no longer desired?

As a man thinks, his actions will follow. So, my question to myself is, "How do I change and challenge your perspective of marriage or love?" It's difficult when you start to realize that you do not know how to love others truly or how to properly display or receive love when you've been taught that showing love or emotions is a sign of weakness. Or that love is normally a one-way street that leads to a dead end.

For a long time, I used to be scared of the word marriage. The traditional definition of the word marriage is "the legally or formally recognized union of two people as partners in a personal relationship."[2] For a long time, my definition of marriage was a short-term legal argument that has a high probability of ending in divorce. Growing up, the only marriages that I ever encountered were broken marriages that led to family drama, bitterness, and financial bondage. My personal experience with unhealthy relationships created a negative perspective and detrimental mindset about marriage—it was seen as the unknown because it was rarely visible or ever spoken. I remember having a serious conversation about marriage with my friends, and during this conversation, I could not stop laughing about the possibility of getting married. Maybe I was laughing out of fear because failure was the outcome for most individuals who went through this journey before me.

Marriage just seems to be far-fetched. I desired to be married, but I thought that everything had to be perfect before saying the words, "I do." Looking for this perfect love made marriage seem

---

[2] Google search. Google. Accessed May 2022. https://www.google.com/search?client=firefox-b-1-d&q=marriage#

more like a mandate instead of an opportunity to explore life with that special someone you trust. Marriage was viewed more like a job that was impossible to achieve or maintain. I understand nothing in life comes easy, and you have to work hard for the things you desire. The world seems to desire everything but real relationships. We glorified cheating, fighting, sex, and independence so much that marriage is no longer wanted? Lately, I have been asking myself, "How do I change my perspective on marriage?" I am learning that it starts with identifying your personal views on marriage, not the world's view on marriage. I will refuse to fall into this false image of relationship goals that is portrayed on social media. It is time to rewrite the narrative surrounding my life.

ABOUT THE AUTHOR:

Social Media:

IG @robertyree3000

FB @robertyree

Email robertyree123@gmail.com

Robert Tyree grew up in Hagerstown, Maryland, in 1985. He is a Baltimore City School System teacher and a basketball coach and a skills trainer. Robert is also a Community Outreach Activator for Unboxing Change and the visionary behind The Refresh Project in Baltimore, Maryland.

REFERENCES

Google search. Google. Accessed May 2022.
https://www.google.com/search?client=firefox-b-1-
d&q=failure.

Google search. Google. Accessed May 2022.
https://www.google.com/search?client=firefox-b-1-
d&q=marriage#

ABOUT THE LEAD AUTHOR

My name is Kenneth Wilson, and I am a native of Silver Spring, MD. I am the Founder and CEO of Men of Stature and Black Squirrel Media. I have professional experience in business, education, politics, and public safety. I am also a passionate community advocate who has worked with people globally.

As a consultant, I have worked with businesses, non-profit organizations, churches, and political outfits all over the world. I have developed programs that have helped dozens of aspiring entrepreneurs begin and pursue their business dreams.

I also have a passion to be a voice in our community, which includes hosting several podcasts and virtual shows. I can be heard weekly as Co-Host of the Community Coalition Show, Reason & Rhyme Podcast, and The Speakeasy Show.

As a public speaker, I discuss issues involving the Black community, with a focus on Black men. I also discuss and teach seminars on business development. In the field of safety, I am a certified CPR/First Aid Instructor. I teach courses in person and virtually.

Accomplishments

- 2016 President's Lifetime Achievement Award Winner
- Two-time Bestselling Author
- Founder and CEO of Black Squirrel Media & Men of Stature
- Creator of the B.LIT Festival & Black Squirrel Media Network

International Safety Expert and Community Advocate

Social Media:

IG @mrkennethwilson

FB @kenneth.wilson.52643

Email kennywilson65@gmail.com

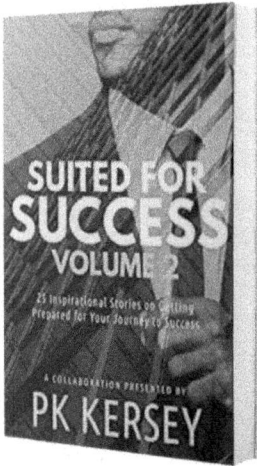

**SUITED FOR SUCCESS:
VOLUME 2**

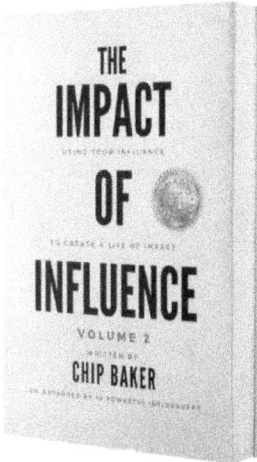

**THE IMPACT OF INFLUENCE:
VOLUME 2**

www.ingramcontent.com/pod-product-compliance
Lightning Source LLC
Chambersburg PA
CBHW070125030426
42335CB00016B/2274